African American Entrepreneurs

✦

BLACK ✦ STARS

AFRICAN AMERICAN ENTREPRENEURS

JIM HASKINS

John Wiley & Sons, Inc.
New York • Chichester • Weinheim • Brisbane • Singapore • Toronto

Copyright © 1998 by Jim Haskins

Published by John Wiley & Sons, Inc.
Design and production by Navta Associates, Inc.

Library of Congress Cataloging-in-Publication Data

Haskins, James.
    African American entrepreneurs / Jim Haskins.
      p.   cm. — (Black stars series)
    Includes index.
    Summary: Profiles a variety of African American entrepreneurs, from the early years, through the Civil War and Reconstruction, to modern times.
    ISBN 0–471–14576–9 (cloth : alk. paper)
    1. Afro-American businesspeople—Biography—Juvenile literature.
[1. Afro-American businesspeople.   2. Afro-Americans—Biography.]
I. Title.   II. Series.
HC102.5.A2H37   1998   97–37389

To Michael, Marcus, and Margaret

CONTENTS

INTRODUCTION

✦

The more than thirty people profiled in the next pages are just a sample of the many clever and skilled African Americans who have beaten the odds and succeeded in business. They are men and women who represent three centuries of black success. The actual number of successful African American entrepreneurs, particularly in modern times, could fill many more such collections.

Africans arrived in North America with many strong traditions, including clever business practices. As far back as 3000 B.C., Nubian traders had prospered selling ebony, gold, cattle, and ivory to Egyptians. In the fifth century A.D., the African kingdom of Ghana was known far and wide for its iron industry and was trading more gold than any other civilization of the time. But in North America, slavery and white prejudices against free blacks prevented most African Americans from continuing their business traditions.

In 1788, J. P. Brissot de Warville, a Frenchman traveling in America, wrote that "if . . . Negroes here are limited to the small retail trade, let us not attribute it to their lack of ability, but rather to the prejudices of the whites who put obstacles in their way."

1

Chief among those obstacles in 1788, and for nearly another century, was slavery. Even those blacks who were free faced nearly insurmountable barriers. They were denied an education and barred by law or custom from equal jobs, credit at banks, and other means for success in business. Forced to devote all their energies to sheer survival, most had few chances to use their intelligence or skills for anything else. Those who did could enrich themselves, buy freedom for themselves and their families, or help fight slavery.

After the Civil War and the Emancipation Proclamation, African Americans had greater opportunities to become entrepreneurs. What does an entrepreneur do? With boldness, initiative, skill, and luck, entrepreneurs see people's needs and start businesses to fill them.

By 1900, scores of black Americans owned small businesses. In that same year, the renowned educator Booker T. Washington formed the National Black Business League at a convention attended by some 400 blacks from thirty states.

Between 1900 and World War I, the number of black businesses more than doubled, from 10,000 to 25,000. In the same period of time, black banks increased in number from four to fifty-one. By 1929, the League estimated that 65,000 blacks owned businesses in the United States.

For a while, that number continued to grow, despite the obstacles that discrimination and segregation represented. In fact, in some cases segregation by law or custom aided black businesspeople, for black consumers were denied service at white business establishments. Ironically, the civil rights movement and federal laws outlawing segregation meant the death of some black businesses, as formerly segregated businesses opened their doors to black consumers.

Beginning in the 1960s, the government helped many blacks to start new businesses or improve enterprises they had already begun. In the 1980s, government support waned. But today there are few areas of enterprise in which blacks are not represented. Even though age-old prejudice and lack of equal opportunity continue to place obstacles in the way, there are now over 600,000 black-owned businesses in the United States.

Today, as in the past, it takes a determined individual to be a successful entrepreneur. As the biographical sketches in the following pages show, there have been many such stars in African American history.

PART ONE

✦

THE
EARLY YEARS

MARIE-THÉRÈSE
METOYER

(1742–1816)

✦

Blacks were entrepreneurs in America from very early times. Years before the Declaration of Independence, one of the most successful of all was born. Marie-Thérèse Metoyer took her first breath in Natchitoches, Louisiana, when Louisiana was still a French colony. Known as Coincoin, a name given to second-born daughters by the Ewe people of western Africa, she probably had at least one parent who was an Ewe. Her parents, François and Françoise, were slaves and had been married in Natchitoches. In the French colonies, slave marriages were legal.

Coincoin's family was owned by Louis Juchereau de Saint-Denis, a commandant in the French army and founder of the army post where they lived. When he died, his ownership of Coincoin passed on to his widow and then to his son, who gave her to his daughter, Marie. During those years, Coincoin gave birth to five children, each one baptized in the Catholic Church. All were sold away from her, but she never forgot them.

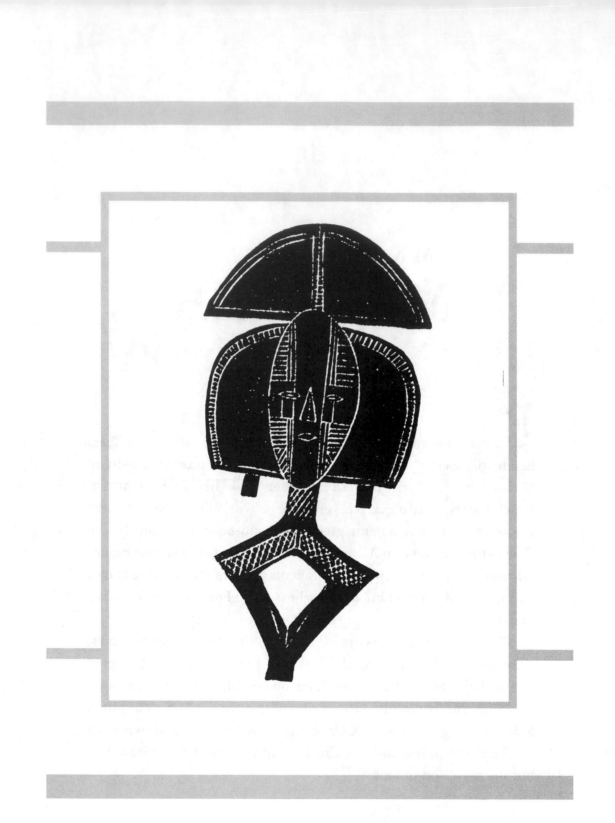

Marie de Saint-Denis rented Coincoin to Claude-Thomas-Pierre Metoyer, a French merchant on Isle Brevelle in the Red River valley of Louisiana. Watching Coincoin toil as a servant in his household, Metoyer fell in love with her, and together they had four children. Eventually Metoyer purchased and freed her, along with their newborn child. She remained with him another eight years, bearing three more children—all legally free because she was now free, too.

In 1786, Claude-Thomas-Pierre Metoyer married someone else. But first he arranged for Coincoin to receive a small plot of land and an annual sum to support herself and her children who were free. At the age of forty-four, Coincoin began a new life. One of the first things

FREEDOM FOR...WHOM?

While building her ranch, Coincoin became a slaveowner herself. Freed blacks were often permitted to purchase slaves who were not family members, but they were not always allowed to set them free. Coincoin probably provided better food, clothes, and protection for her slaves than other owners might have. Still, it seems strange that someone who loved freedom so much had slaves of her own.

It is impossible to know what was in Coincoin's mind, but it is likely that she had several reasons for owning slaves. Most practically, she needed the help. There may not have been enough freed blacks in the area to hire, and she certainly could not have hired white help. She may also have concluded that owning slaves would make whites believe that she supported slavery. Whites, sometimes with good reason, suspected freed blacks of aiding slave insurrections. They would have no suspicions against someone who also owned slaves.

By the time of Coincoin's death in 1816 at the age of seventy-four, she owned sixteen slaves. Coincoin's descendants inherited her energy, spirit, and talent for business. Before the Civil War, they built an agricultural empire on Isle Brevelle that included nearly 20,000 acres of land, a dozen homes, and, ironically, 500 slaves.

Within 400 years, more than 15 million Africans were captured and shipped to the New World. Those who survived the passage—and their children from generation to generation—were sold like cattle to the highest bidders. (Library of Congress)

she did was to purchase her eldest daughter, Marie-Louise. She had been crippled in a shooting accident and cost only $300. Coincoin's plan was to buy back all of her other enslaved children, but first she had to make more money.

Coincoin planted tobacco and indigo and raised cattle and turkeys, all of which she sold. She also trapped bear and sold their hides and grease.

In 1762, France ceded a large part of Louisiana Province to Spain, including all territory west of the Mississippi River. By 1794, Coincoin had established herself financially and secured land from the Spanish government. Coincoin obtained a grant of 640 acres of piney woods on Isle Brevelle. There she herded cattle and raised crops, profiting handsomely from her hard work and smart business practices.

Now she could purchase more of her children. They were scattered throughout western Louisiana and eastern Texas. She would have to travel to find them and negotiate their sale. Nearly all their owners were willing to sell them, for cash or on credit. Sadly, one daughter, Françoise, was not obtainable, but Coincoin and her heirs managed to purchase Françoise's children.

> ◆ To **negotiate** means to arrive at an agreement with another person.

In 1802, at the age of sixty, Coincoin offered to forfeit the annual payment Metoyer gave her in exchange for the freedom of their first three children. Metoyer agreed, and Coincoin at last realized her dream of freedom for her entire family.

Coincoin's home on Isle Brevelle, Melrose Plantation, still stands. It has been designated a National Historic Landmark.

PAUL
CUFFE

(1759–1817)

✦

Unlike Marie-Thérèse Metoyer, Paul Cuffe was born free. In 1795, he sailed his 69-ton schooner *Ranger* into Norfolk, Virginia, to purchase a cargo of corn. He later wrote in his autobiography of the day the ship dropped anchor and he and his crew of blacks went ashore: "The people were filled with astonishment and alarm. A vessel owned and commanded by a black man, and manned with a crew of the same complexion, was unprecedented and surprising. The white inhabitants were struck with apprehensions of the injurious effects on the minds of their slaves, suspecting that he [Cuffe] wished secretly to kindle the spirit of rebellion, and excite a destructive revolt among them."[1]

Cuffe was angered by this kind of reaction. He was one of the few black men of his time to own a ship. But he did not let the concerns of whites—in Norfolk or elsewhere—interfere with his plans. He went about his business, purchased his cargo, and set sail for Connecticut, his home.

Paul Cuffe was born on the island of Cuttyhunk, off the coast of New Bedford, Massachusetts. He was the seventh of ten children of Cuffe Slocum and his wife, Ruth Moses, a Wampanoag Indian. Cuffe Slocum had been born in Africa and brought to the North American colonies as a slave. But he had managed to purchase his freedom from his master in Dartmouth, Massachusetts, and his children were born free.

Cuffe Slocum died when Paul was only thirteen. Although still a boy, Paul knew he would have to provide for himself. First, he found a tutor and learned to read and write. Then he studied navigation. At the age of sixteen, he went to sea, shipping out on a whaler bound for the Gulf of Mexico.

During Cuffe's third voyage, in 1776, the Revolutionary War broke out. His ship was captured by the British, and he spent three months in a New York prison. Cuffe settled in Westport, Connecticut, after his release from prison. Because going to sea during the war was hazardous, he worked as a hired hand on a farm. Meanwhile, he continued to study navigation and to look for ways to make a better living. He and his brother, John, built an open boat with which they could trade with towns on the Connecticut shore, but rough seas and pirates loyal to England made that entrepreneurial venture too dangerous. The brothers returned to laboring on a farm as the war continued.

Paul Cuffe was still determined to make a living as a merchant mariner. Twice, he built small boats and attempted to trade. His first boat was seized by American pirates who supported the British. During his second attempt, he failed to sell his cargo of goods. Finally, on his third attempt, he managed to make such a good profit that he was able to buy an 18-ton craft and hire help.

A few years after the Revolutionary War, Cuffe married Alice Pequit, who, like his mother, was a Wampanoag Indian. He rented a small house in Westport and used his new boat to sail to Ontario,

The Spirit of 1776

The Cuffes were keenly aware that one reason behind the revolt of the colonies against England was the charge of "no taxation without representation." If the colonists refused to pay taxes to England because they had no say in how the English government was conducted, why should the Cuffes pay taxes to the state of Connecticut? As black men, they could not legally vote or own a business, so they refused to pay taxes. When state authorities arrived to seize the Cuffes' property, they found none to seize. In December 1780, Paul and John Cuffe were jailed for nonpayment of taxes.

Released from prison the following spring, the Cuffes pursued their cause, putting the issue before a town meeting in Taunton, Connecticut, where they had been jailed. The Cuffes, along with five other blacks, demanded that free Negroes have the same rights as whites to own businesses and vote or else be relieved of taxation. The Cuffes finally had to pay the taxes they owed, but they had put up a courageous fight for the same rights for which the white colonists had gone to war.

Canada, where he bought a cargo of dried codfish. Back home, he sold his cargo quickly.

Over the next ten years, often in partnership with one of his brothers-in-law, Michael Wainer, also a seaman, Cuffe made ever greater profits and built ever larger vessels.

He then entered the expanding whaling business, sailing on the 42-ton schooner *Mary* in 1793. He personally harpooned two whales. He then traveled to Philadelphia to exchange whale oil and bone for hardware to outfit the *Ranger*, the 69-ton schooner that he piloted to Norfolk, Virginia, on what was probably his first trip south.

Cuffe took the corn he bought in Virginia and sold it in Westport. When the market for corn was not good, he dealt in gypsum, a mineral used in the making of plaster. He traded in whatever commodity would bring him profits. Cuffe's longest voyage of trade was on the

268-ton *Alpha*. With its black crew of seven, he sailed south to Wilmington and Savannah, then across the ocean to Helsingör, Denmark, and Göteborg, Sweden, and returned to Philadelphia with passengers and freight.

By the time Captain Paul Cuffe was fifty years old, he owned a small fleet of ships. He built a schoolhouse for Westport with his own money on his own land and then donated both land and building "freely…to the use of the public."[2]

✦ A **commodity** is a product, something useful or valuable that you can trade.

✦ **Markets** are the public places where buyers and sellers come together or the opportunities they create for buying and selling their products.

Every year, however, he became more and more outraged over slavery, which he described as the "evil of one brother making merchandise of and holding his brother in bondage." He eventually decided that the best course for freed slaves was to return to their native Africa. One day in the fall of 1810, he and a crew of nine black seamen set sail for Sierra Leone in western Africa. He stayed there three months, taking notes on the country's possibilities as a home for blacks from North America. He made one more visit to Sierra Leone before returning there in 1815 on the *Traveller* with thirty-eight black emigrants and a cargo of supplies to get them started in their new home. Cuffe's health soon failed, and he died in October 1817. His dreams of an African nation of black emigrants from America would be carried forth by others and bear fruit in the settling of Liberia by African American freedmen in 1821. But there would never be a large exodus of free blacks from the United States. Free people of color in Richmond, Virginia, even declared in January 1817 that they preferred to be "colonized in the most remote corner of the land of our nativity, to being exiled" in Africa.[3]

Cuffe Farm at 1504 Drift Road in Westport, Connecticut, is now a National Historic Landmark.

JAMES
FORTEN

(1766–1842)

✦

J ames Forten knew Paul Cuffe as an adult, and like Cuffe, Forten was filled with the revolutionary spirit of his times.

Forten was born free in Philadelphia. His father, Thomas Forten, had also been freeborn and had purchased his wife's freedom with his wages as a sailmaker in the employ of Robert Bridges. James Forten was only seven when his father fell to his death while working on the tall sails of a ship. His family survived the sudden tragedy, and life went on.

James Forten attended a Quaker school as a boy. The colony of Pennsylvania had been established by the Quakers, a religious sect formally known as the Society of Friends. The Quakers believed in the equality of all people and had early on allowed blacks to attend their schools.

After the Revolutionary War, Forten became an apprentice to Robert Bridges, the Philadelphia sailmaker who had employed his father. Forten was such a

✦ An **apprentice** is a person who learns a skill by working under someone who is already trained and knows what to do.

THE PATRIOT

At the age of fourteen, Forten enlisted in the navy, where he served as a powder boy, loading cannons aboard the *Royal Lewis*, a privateer, or private ship commissioned by the American navy. The *Royal Lewis* was captured by the British navy, and its crew, which included some twenty blacks, was taken as prisoners. Forten became friends with the British captain's son. The boy asked Forten to go back to England with him to live a life of wealth and aristocratic privilege.

Forten paused and answered, "I am a prisoner here for the liberties of my country. I never, never shall prove a traitor to her interests."[1] He was transferred to the British prison ship *Jersey* and later released in a general prisoner exchange.

skilled and responsible worker that by 1786 he had been named foreman of the sailmaking loft. Twelve years later, in 1798, he became its owner. More than forty workers, both black and white, were employed in his factory.

Sometime after 1800, Forten invented a device that helped control the sails on ships and that opened the door to the modern sailing industry. The exact date is not known because Forten never patented his invention. He secured contracts from the United States Navy to outfit its vessels, and he quietly made a fortune.

Forten could have made even more money had he been willing to work with the slave traders. But he refused to outfit slave vessels with sail rigging or with his sail-handling device. Instead, he used much of his wealth in good causes. For instance, he joined other black Philadelphia businessmen in various endeavors to help the poor. He gave a lot of money to support the *Liberator*, an anti-slavery newspaper founded by William Lloyd Garrison, and he helped to build its subscription list. A strong supporter of the United States government, his largest customer, he helped to recruit black soldiers to serve in the War of 1812.

Forten's friends asked him to be chairman of the Colored People's Convention, which met at Bethel Church in Philadelphia on August 10, 1817. Forten, along with 3,000 others, adopted this basic resolution: "We will never separate ourselves voluntarily from the slave population of this country; they are our brethren by ties of [shared blood], suffering and wrong; we feel there is more virtue in suffering privation with them, than fancied advantage for a reason."[2]

Forten was not in favor of colonization in Africa. "We are contented in the land that gave us birth and for which many of our fathers fought and died," he said. He had more faith in offering money to master mechanics to take black children as apprentices than in settling another country.[3]

At Forten's death in 1842, his sail loft enterprise was estimated to be worth $100,000, a vast sum for any American at that time.

PIERRE
TOUSSAINT

(1766–1853)

✦

As successful in his time and place as James Forten was, Pierre Toussaint, like Forten, began his entrepreneurial life as an apprentice.

Toussaint was born a slave on a plantation in Haiti when that island was a French possession prized for its sugarcane crop. A house servant, Toussaint was encouraged to read and write and was treated well by his owners, the wealthy and aristocratic Jean and Marie Bérard. But the cruelty of other slaveowners led to unrest in Haiti. The Bérards, accompanied by Toussaint, fled to New York. Fully expecting the slave revolt in Haiti to be put down by French troops, Jean Bérard had brought only enough money to maintain his family comfortably in New York for one year.

Soon after settling in a rented house on Reade Street, Jean Bérard apprenticed twenty-one-year-old Toussaint to a Mr. Merchant, one of the city's leading hairdressers. Toussaint quickly mastered the art of making the elaborate hairstyles that were in vogue for wealthy women, but he had to walk to their homes to do his work, because blacks were not allowed to ride the city's public horsecars.

The situation in Haiti grew worse. Frightened by the rumors of impending disaster, Jean Bérard sailed to Haiti to save his property. Bérard never returned to New York; he died of pleurisy, a disease of the lungs, on his plantation. Not long after his death, his plantation was destroyed. Although French troops eventually put down the rebellion, the French hold on the island had been broken. In 1803, Haiti became an independent black republic.

Having barely adjusted to the news of Jean's death and the conditions in Haiti, Marie Bérard learned that her husband's investments in a New York City business were wiped out when the firm collapsed. Penniless, she asked Toussaint to sell some of her jewelry. He refused, offering instead to provide for the household's weekly expenses. He sometimes earned $1,000 per year per client at a time when a man was considered wealthy if he made $10,000 a year.

Although he had every right to be free, Toussaint was sensitive to Madame Bérard's feelings and to appearances, and he always acted the dutiful slave. Marie Bérard remarried, but her new husband, Gabriel Nicolas, also a refugee French planter from Haiti, suffered financial reverses. Pierre Toussaint continued to support the household. In fact, he put off his own plans to marry a young Haitian girl, Juliette Nöcl, because he felt that he could not marry her while he was responsible for the Nicolas household.

Marie Nicolas died when Toussaint was forty-five years old. On her deathbed, she informed him that she had provided for his freedom in a legal document dated July 2, 1807.

Pierre Toussaint wasted no time in marrying Juliette, but otherwise, he continued to live much as he always had, attending early mass each morning before he went to work. He used his money to help the poor. He provided much of the support for the Prince Street Orphanage, New York's first Catholic institution for homeless children, and he helped raise funds to build St. Patrick's Cathedral and St. Vincent de Paul Church.

Pierre and Juliette took orphans into their home. Toussaint also put his life on the line to nurse victims of cholera and yellow fever, crossing quarantine barriers to reach sufferers in the city's early ghettoes. He continued to work well into his later years. One of his customers said, "Toussaint, you are the richest man I know. Why not stop working?" Toussaint replied, "Then, Madame, I should not have enough for others."[1] He continued to work until Juliette died in 1851. Not long afterward, Toussaint himself became ill. He died on June 30, 1853, at the age of eighty-seven.

Pierre Toussaint was first buried in the cemetery of Old St. Patrick's Church on Mott Street. His remains now lie in a crypt beneath the floor of St. Patrick's Cathedral on Fifth Avenue in New York City. Catholic church officials had come to believe that the good man they reburied there was very likely a saint.

"FREE FRANK"
McWORTER

(1777–1854)

◆

Frank McWorter built an entire town in the pursuit of complete freedom for his family. He was born a slave in Union County, South Carolina, a frontier outpost. His mother, Juda, had been born in western Africa. Evidence indicates that Juda's owner, George McWhorter, was Frank's father.

Around 1795, George McWhorter purchased land in Pulaski County, Kentucky, some two hundred miles northwest of Union County, South Carolina. Kentucky law stated that in order to own the land, the buyer must live on it, fence two acres, and cultivate a crop of corn. So George McWhorter sent eighteen-year-old Frank and three other McWhorter slaves to Kentucky to establish his claim to the land.

During that year in Kentucky, Frank met Lucy, who belonged to William Denham, a relative of the McWhorters. Four years later Frank and Lucy chose to be man and wife, although slaves in Kentucky were not allowed to marry. Because their respective masters lived some distance away from each other, Frank and Lucy were unable to live together under a single roof. Over the course of the next eighteen

years, however, they had thirteen children, all of them the legal property of Lucy's owner.

The years passed. They were hard but never boring. Frank got George McWhorter's permission to hire out his own time as a jack-of-all-trades, agreeing to pay an annual fee for the privilege. After George moved his family south to Wayne County and left Frank in charge of the Pulaski County farm, Frank had even more time to work for himself. But it was the War of 1812 that led him to establish his own business.

In its fight against Great Britain, the United States needed huge quantities of saltpeter, the principal ingredient in gunpowder. Kentucky was the nation's leading producer of saltpeter, and the Rockcastle caves, rich in potassium nitrate, or niter, saltpeter's basic ingredient, were only a short distance away from the McWhorter farm in Pulaski County. Frank worked the farm by day and devoted his nights to mining and producing saltpeter. After the War of 1812, as the demand for saltpeter declined, Frank also went into the business of making salt. In those days, salt-making even on a small scale could be profitable.

George McWhorter died in 1815. Before his death, he had promised to free Frank, but he had made no provision in his will for Frank's emancipation. McWhorter's heirs agreed to free Frank, on payment of $500, more money than Frank had yet saved. That year, Lucy gave birth to their thirteenth child, Solomon. By 1817, she was pregnant again. Frank did not want his fourteenth child born in slavery, and by then he had earned enough to buy Lucy's freedom. He purchased her for $800. As a consequence, their child, Squire, born the following September, was the first member of their family to be born free.

In 1819, Frank purchased himself, paying $800. His owners had decided to raise his price! No matter. Rather than choose a surname, he proudly had his name listed as Free Frank in the 1820 census. From then on, Frank paid whatever price freedom demanded.

Ten years later, in 1829, Free Frank purchased freedom for his twenty-five-year-old son, Frank Junior, by trading his saltpeter works to the Denham family. Three years earlier, young Frank had escaped and made it safely to Canada. But Free Frank wanted his son with him, and so he bought his freedom.

Now that Free Frank had traded away his main source of income, he had little reason to stay in Kentucky. It was no longer a frontier. In 1830, he sold the land he had acquired and moved the free members of his family—Frank Junior and Squire, Commodore, and Lucy Ann, three children who had been born free after 1817—to Illinois, a free state. They traveled by ox-drawn wagon, crossed the Ohio River on a flatboat, and settled in Hadley Township in Pike County, on the Illinois frontier.

By the time they reached Illinois, Free Frank and his family had dropped the "h" in their last name and were known as the McWorters. The family, who at the time were the only blacks in Pike County, bought land and began to raise hogs and horses for cash money to buy Frank and Lucy's children who remained in slavery.

Four years later, in 1835, Frank purchased his son Solomon for $550. Two daughters and their children remained in slavery. (Frank and Lucy's other slave children had died by this time.) Money was scarce, and time seemed to be running out.

Then Free Frank had his best moneymaking idea yet. He decided to establish a town, primarily because selling lots was the best way to obtain cash money. He bought land and had it surveyed, or plotted. He named the town New Philadelphia. Free Frank was a deeply religious man, and it is possible that he took the name from a passage in Revelation, in which God says: "To the angel of the church in Philadelphia. . . . I know your deeds; that is why I have left before you an open door which no one can close."[1]

New Philadelphia was one of six towns founded by single proprietors in Pike County at that time. Free Frank quickly opened a store

Trying to get ahead, thousands of African Americans like the McWorters headed to the next frontier to earn money, their freedom, or both. Most became merchants, farmers, or cowboys. During the 1849 Gold Rush, some like this miner went all the way to California to seek their fortune. (Schomburg Center for Research in Black Culture)

UNDERCOVER WITH THE UNDERGROUND RAILROAD

The Underground Railroad, an informal network of blacks and whites who helped escaped slaves from the South reach freedom in Canada, was active by the 1840s. In New Philadelphia, the McWorters aided many fugitives. They built a secret room in the basement of their home as a hiding place, and McWorter's sons often helped lead the fugitives to Canada.

and worked with county officials to build cross-county roads nearby. He had sold eight town lots by 1841; the purchasers included whites. With the increased prosperity of the county in the middle 1840s, New Philadelphia grew. Soon it had a stagecoach stop and a post office.

By 1850, Free Frank and his family owned over 600 acres of land valued at more than $7,000. Only 3,000 of the nation's nearly 440,000 free blacks owned land. In that year, Free Frank purchased two of his grandchildren and the wife of his son Squire. By 1854, he had purchased four more family members.

Free Frank McWorter died on September 7, 1854, at the age of seventy-seven. He had not lived to accomplish his dream of freeing his entire family, but his will provided for his work to go on. His sons carried out his wishes, and within three years they purchased a total of seven more grandchildren and great-grandchildren. Altogether, fifteen members of the Frank McWorter family were freed from bondage, at a cost of more than $14,000.

THOMAS L.
JENNINGS

(1791–1859)

✦

While slaves and freemen such as Free Frank McWorter were taking advantage of the few opportunities available to them in the South and Midwest, enterprising African Americans in the cities of the Northeast were also finding ways to prosper. They, too, faced extraordinary obstacles. As Edgar J. McManus wrote in *A History of Negro Slavery in New York*, blacks were "in a very real sense a population in quarantine, trapped in a system of racial bondage in many ways as cruel and intolerable as slavery."[1] But many within the city's small, cultured black middle class managed to thrive.

Thomas L. Jennings of New York City was one of them. He operated a boarding house, but his tailoring and dry cleaning business brought him more success. In 1821, at the age of thirty, he patented a dry cleaning process known as "dry scouring." Jennings is believed to be the first African American to have received a patent for an invention.

The first U.S. Patent Act had been enacted in 1790, one year before Jennings was born. It was meant to encourage innovation by making

Negroes for Sale.

A Cargo of very fine stout Men and Women, in good order and fit for immediate service, just imported from the Windward Coast of Africa, in the Ship Two Brothers.—Conditions are one half Cash or Produce, the other half payable the first of January next, giving Bond and Security if required.

The Sale to be opened at 10 o'Clock each Day, in Mr. Bourdeaux's Yard, at No, 48, on the Bay.

May 19, 1784.   JOHN MITCHELL.

Thirty Seasoned Negroes

To be Sold for Credit, at Private Sale.

AMONGST which is a Carpenter, none of whom are known to be dishonest.

Also, to be sold for Cash, a regular bred young Negroe Man-Cook, born in this Country, who served several Years under an exceeding good French Cook abroad, and his Wife a middle aged Washer-Woman, (both very honest) and their two Children. Likewise, a young Man a Carpenter. For Terms apply to the Printer.

detailed information about inventions known to the public. It also protected the inventor from unauthorized use of his or her invention. The patent office did not keep records of an inventor's race. There may have been earlier inventions patented by black people, but Jennings's is the first to be verified. He received his patent on March 3, 1821.

Jennings used the profits from his successful businesses to support many causes. Abolitionism, or the movement to abolish slavery, was one of the most important to him. The first abolition society was formed in Philadelphia in 1775. The Declaration of Independence and the creation of the new nation based on the idea that all men were created equal brought the issue of slavery to the forefront. Those who were against slavery demanded its end. Inspired by the great religious revival that swept the country in the early part of the nineteenth century, with its moral urgency to end sinful practices and its vision of human perfection, abolitionists declared that slavery was a moral evil that had to be wiped out.

Jennings was a leading member of the National Colored Convention Movement, whose first Annual Convention of the People of Color was held at Wesleyan Church in Philadelphia on September 15, 1831. Its purpose was to "devise ways and means for the bettering of our condition."[2] He was also a founder of the first black organization, the New York African Society for Mutual Relief, chartered on March 23, 1810, whose purpose was to raise funds to aid the widows and orphans of its deceased members.

He attended Abyssinian Baptist Church, which in the next century would have the largest black congregation in New York City and be the political power base of its pastor, the Reverend Adam Clayton Powell Jr., who served in Congress from 1945 to 1970.

Jennings was proud of his race and thought he was as much an American as any other citizen of the still-new United States. Like James Forten in Philadelphia, he was against the idea of black American emigration to Africa. At a meeting of the New York African

Society for Mutual Relief in 1828, Jennings said: "Our claims are on America; it is the land that gave us birth. We know no other country. It is a land in which our fathers have suffered and toiled. They have watered it with their tears and fanned it with their sighs.

"Our relation with Africa is the same as the white man's is with Europe. We have passed through several generations in this country and consequently have become naturalized. Our habits, our manners, our passions, our dispositions have become the same. The same mother's milk has nourished us both in infancy; the white child and the colored have both hung on the same breast. I might as well tell the white man about England, France or Spain, the country from whence his forefathers emigrated, and call him a European, as for him to call us Africans. Africa is as foreign to us as Europe is to them."[3]

Jennings and his wife lived at 167 Church Street, and they had several children. Thomas L. Jennings Jr. studied dentistry in Boston and established a practice in New Orleans. Matilda Jennings, a dressmaker, married and lived in San Francisco.

In 1854, Jennings's sister, Elizabeth, brought suit against the Third Avenue Railway Company for discrimination after a conductor put her off a train reserved for whites. Her lawyer was young Chester A. Arthur, fresh out of law school. His law firm, Culver, Parker, and Arthur, had established a reputation for handling abolitionist causes and believed Elizabeth had a strong case.

Thomas L. Jennings spearheaded the fundraising drive to pay Elizabeth's legal costs. One of his appeals, addressed "To the Citizens of Color, Male and Female, of the City and State of New York," pointed out that no actual law forced persons of African descent to ride in segregated trolley cars marked COLORED and that it was really a matter of custom, tradition, and transit company rules. The case, the appeal went on, "will bring up the whole question of our right...in the public conveyances."[4] In winning her suit, Elizabeth effectively ended discrimination in transportation in New York City. Chester A. Arthur went on to become president of the United States.

Thomas L. Jennings died in 1859, four years after his sister won her case.

WILLIAM A.
LEIDESDORFF

(1810–1848)

✦

The only individual in this collection to inherit wealth, William Alexander Leidesdorff, was born in Concordia on the island of St. Croix in the Danish West Indies (now the U.S. Virgin Islands). He had a Danish father and an African mother named Anna Marie Sparks. He had a privileged childhood on his wealthy father's plantation, and although no record of his education exists, he became fluent in several languages, including French and German.

As a young man, Leidesdorff worked in his father's cotton business, sailing ships to such ports as New York City and New Orleans. Reportedly, a failed love affair spurred Leidesdorff to set out for California. His ship, the *Julia Ann*, arrived in Yerba Buena (later renamed San Francisco), via New Orleans in 1841.

He soon made Yerba Buena his home, established himself in trade with Hawaii, and purchased two 300-foot lots on the corner of Clay and Kearney Streets. He later built Yerba Buena's first hotel on that property.

With the aim of obtaining additional large land grants from

◆ William A. Leidesdorff ◆

Mexico, Leidesdorff became a naturalized Mexican citizen in 1844 and acquired from the Mexican government a 35,000-acre estate, which he named Rio Del Rancho Americano. There, he raised cattle and horses, and by 1846, he had 4,500 head of cattle and 250 horses.

Also in 1846, he obtained a grant for a lot at the foot of California Street in Yerba Buena, renamed San Francisco that same year. Here, he built a warehouse for the export of tallow, which was used in the making of candles, and of hides, which were used to make clothing and shoes. The following year, he acquired property on Montgomery Street, near California Street, and built a home.

His entrepreneurial ventures became legendary. He purchased a 37-foot steamboat, *Sitka*, to operate for commercial purposes on San Francisco Bay. It was the first steamboat ever seen in that bay, and Leidesdorff became known as the "Robert Fulton of the West." He hosted the first recorded public horse race in California—in a meadow near Mission Dolores. In 1845, even though Leidesdorff was a Mexican citizen, the U.S. consul to Mexico, Colonel Thomas David Larkin, appointed him vice-consul, making Leidesdorff probably the first black diplomat in the history of the United States.

Leidesdorff held that position in 1846 when the American explorer John C. Frémont led American settlers to set up a republic at Sonoma. Leidesdorff supported Frémont. Meanwhile, Mexico and the United States had gone to war, although the news had not yet reached California. The *Californios* in the north supported the United States' effort and worked with the U.S. troops who arrived to occupy the main population centers. Leidesdorff arranged a fancy dress ball at his home to entertain the American leaders.

Inhabitants of southern California were not as cooperative as those in the north. In fact, they resisted U.S. forces until 1847, when they were defeated. Mexico formally ceded California to the United States

Go West, Young Man

Originally part of New Spain, as the Spanish empire in the Americas was called, California had been colonized by Spain. The settlers were known as the *Californios*. The *Californios* built missions supposedly for the purpose of bringing Christianity to the native Indians, whom they forced to work as manual laborers.

Mexico won its independence from Spain in 1821 and later took control of California. Under Mexican rule, the native Indians were released from their servitude. Many mission lands were subsequently given to *Californios*, who built vast estates called *ranchos* and raised cattle. Colonization of California was still largely Mexican when William A. Leidesdorff arrived in 1841.

Yerba Buena was a small, sparsely populated port in 1841, but that was soon to change. Founded as a military outpost by Juan Bautista in 1776, it was quickly becoming a popular stopping place for ships on their way to the Far East. Also, the first American immigrants began to arrive in California by overland routes in 1841, and Leidesdorff must have sensed the business opportunities they represented.

the following year; and in 1850, it was admitted to the Union as the thirty-first state.

In 1848, the same year that Mexico ceded California to the United States, gold was discovered in California not far from Leidesdorff's ranch. But Leidesdorff did not live to to take advantage of the new business opportunities it presented. An epidemic of typhus hit the San Francisco area that year, and on May 18 Leidesdorff became one of its victims.

When Leidesdorff died, his estate was deeply in debt. But the later discovery of gold on his ranch made the property very valuable.

Leidesdorff's estate was eventually awarded to a white army captain, Joseph Folsom, who became wealthy as a result.

The high regard in which his fellow San Franciscans held this first black resident of their town is evidenced by the fact that by 1856, a street had been named after him. Three blocks long today, it is, quite fittingly, located in San Francisco's Financial District.

DAVID
RUGGLES

(1810–1849)

✦

Nineteenth-century New York City was America's greatest city. It was also strongly segregated. Out of a population of some 515,000, about 14,000 were of African descent. Blacks were restricted in voting, denied jobs, refused service in restaurants, forbidden to serve as jurors, and excluded from membership in professional organizations. Slavery was abolished in New York State in 1827, but black New Yorkers remained a few steps above slavery.

David Ruggles, the first publisher of an African American magazine, arrived in New York in 1827. Born of free parents in Norwich, Connecticut, on March 15, 1810, he left home at the age of seventeen and moved to New York, where he started a grocery business.

Almost immediately, the abolitionists' campaign against the moral evil of slavery captured the young man's imagination, and he became involved as a traveling agent for the *Emancipator*, their weekly newspaper.

In 1834, Ruggles opened a bookshop and circulating library at 67 Lispenard Street in New York City, thereby becoming the first African

American bookseller. He soon began to publish pamphlets condemning black oppression.

He thrived on fighting for justice. When the New York Committee of Vigilance was founded by leading white and black citizens, Ruggles became its director. The committee helped runaway slaves get settled in New York or travel farther north, to Boston or Providence or Canada. It also watched out for slave hunters and kidnappers, and it gave legal aid to people tried in court as runaways.

The most famous person Ruggles's committee helped was Frederick Douglass, one of the most powerful orators in the cause and a newspaper publisher himself.

THE ABOLITIONIST

Ruggles's anti-slavery activities were apparently too much for some of New York's pro-slavery whites. In the fall of 1835, Ruggles's bookshop was destroyed by fire. It was suspected that pro-slavery whites were responsible. But Ruggles would not be intimidated. The November 24, 1835, issue of the *Emancipator* contained the following advertisement:

> Agency Office, 67 Lispenard Street, New York—The friends of Human rights are respectfully informed that in consequence of the destruction of my books, pamphlets, and stationery by fire, I am compelled for the present to discontinue the sale of books and the circulating library, but will abide in the same place, and continue my agency for all Anti-Slavery Publications.[1]

Less than two months later, an attempt was made to kidnap Ruggles and sell him into slavery. Early one morning, he was awakened by a knock on the door. From the other side, a man who identified himself as "Mr. Nash" claimed he had urgent business with Ruggles. But a suspicious Ruggles refused to open the door. Foiled, the man returned with reinforcements, who battered down the door of the house. By that time, however, Ruggles had escaped.[2]

Ruggles continued to create businesses to help black people. In 1837, he established a newspaper called the *Mirror of Liberty*. The following year, he opened a reading room for blacks at 36 Lispenard Street "because Negroes were not given free privileges in the libraries of New York."[3]

Ruggles edited yet another newspaper, the *Genius of Freedom*, in New York between 1845 and 1847. He died two years later at the age of thirty-nine, nearly fifteen years before slavery was ended in the United States.

PART TWO

THE CIVIL WAR YEARS AND RECONSTRUCTION

ELIZABETH
KECKLEY

(1818–1907)

✦

Elizabeth Keckley was born Elizabeth Hobbs to a slave family in Dinwiddie Courthouse, Virginia. She was only in her mid-teens when she was sold to a slaveowner in North Carolina and forced to leave her family.

In her new place of enslavement in North Carolina, Elizabeth was raped, probably by her owner, and later gave birth to a son. Then, when Elizabeth was eighteen, she and her son were repurchased by the daughter of her original owner, who took them to St. Louis, Missouri, to live.

In all probability, Elizabeth was sought out by a member of her original owner's family because of her exceptional skills as a seamstress. She started a dressmaking business in St. Louis that eventually became so prosperous that it supported her owners and their five children, as well as herself and her own son.

Elizabeth wanted to be free, and one reason why she married James Keckley was because he claimed to be free. She later learned

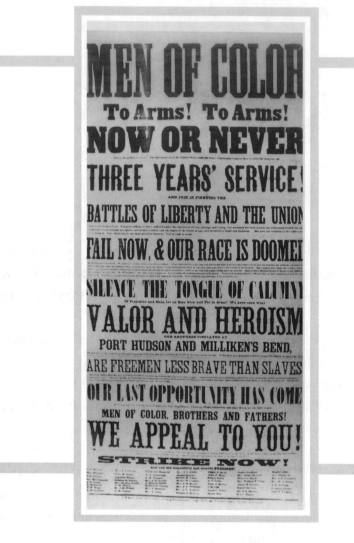

A Civil War Woman

Elizabeth Keckley worked for the abolitionist cause, helping other black women form an organization to aid former slaves seeking refuge in the capital. She secured donations from Mrs. Lincoln as well as from such prominent African American abolitionists as Frederick Douglass and Wendell Phillips. The Contraband Relief Association, as her organization was known, changed its name to the Freedmen and Soldiers' Relief Association of Washington when blacks were allowed to join the army.

Nearly 180,000 blacks fought in the war between the North and the South. Sadly, Keckley's son, who was light-complected enough to serve in a white regiment in the Union Army, was killed in action.

that he had lied to her about his status. The couple separated, but Elizabeth kept his name for the rest of her life.

In 1855, when Elizabeth was thirty-seven years old, she secured loans from her dressmaking clients to purchase her freedom for $1,200. She continued in her dressmaking business in St. Louis for another five years, until she had earned enough money to pay back the loans.

In 1860, Keckley moved first to Baltimore, Maryland, and then to Washington, D.C. She employed twenty girls in her business in the nation's capital, and her clients included Mrs. Jefferson Davis, whose husband was at that time a senator from Mississippi. Introduced to Mary Todd Lincoln on the day after President Lincoln's inauguration, Keckley soon became the First Lady's dressmaker. Within months, seven southern states had seceded from the Union, and Keckley's former client, Mrs. Davis, became the First Lady of the Confederate States of America.

Elizabeth Keckley moved into the White House, serving as Mary Todd Lincoln's dressmaker, personal maid, and confidante. Keckley

Matthew Brady took this formal photograph of Mary Todd Lincoln in 1861, one year after President Lincoln's inauguration. Elizabeth Keckley probably made this gown and styled Mrs. Lincoln's hair for the occasion. (National Archives)

told an interviewer, "I dressed Mrs. Lincoln for every levee. I made every stitch of clothing that she wore. I dressed her hair. I put on her skirts and dresses. I fixed her bouquets, saw that her gloves were all right, and remained with her each evening until Mr. Lincoln came for her. My hands were the last to touch her before she took the arm of Mr.

Lincoln and went forth to meet the ladies and gentlemen on those great occasions."[1]

After President Lincoln was assassinated in 1865, Mary Todd Lincoln and her children moved out of the White House. Keckley moved, too, but continued to make dresses for and remained a close personal friend of Mary Todd Lincoln until 1868.

Mrs. Lincoln was shocked when Keckley's memoir, *Behind the Scenes; or, Thirty Years a Slave, and Four Years in the White House,* was published that year. Written in collaboration with James Redpath, who ran a lecture agency, the book described Keckley's life as a slave and the brutality she'd been forced to endure in North Carolina as well as life at the White House, including the personalities of the Lincolns and their family dynamics. Mary Todd Lincoln considered the book a betrayal of her friendship.

Keckley spent her last years supported by a pension paid to her because her son had died fighting for the Union cause. The rest home in which she died on May 26, 1907, was one she had helped found for others.

In spite of the controversy that raged around it, Keckley's book proved to be a valuable resource for Lincoln scholars. Its accuracy has rarely been questioned.

RICHARD HENRY
BOYD

(1843–1922)

✦

Like Elizabeth Keckley, Richard Boyd was born a slave but rose on the winds of freedom and personal initiative. At his birth on March 15, 1843, in Nexubee County, Mississippi, he was given the name Dick Gray. During the Civil War, he accompanied members of his owner's family into battle. But after emancipation, in 1867, he changed his name to Richard Henry Boyd and set out on his own.

At first, the future entrepreneur became a minister in the predominantly white Texas Baptist Convention of churches. To Boyd, the times probably seemed hopeful, because new laws were passed to give African Americans the right to vote as equals. But events proved otherwise.

In 1870, Boyd organized, largely with his own funds, the first association of African American Baptists in the state of Texas. He started with six churches but steadily built the association until it represented most black Baptist congregations in the state.

By 1896, Boyd had become a real power in both state and national Baptist circles. When the United States and other nations began build-

OUT OF BONDAGE

During the post–Civil War period called Reconstruction (1865–1877), blacks briefly enjoyed the right to vote and hold office. Like most whites, however, members of the Texas Baptist Convention were officially against Reconstruction reforms. But Richard Henry Boyd did not falter in his faith or lose hope. He resisted the racism by forming a separate group for black churches.

ing a canal across the Isthmus of Panama to facilitate shipping between the eastern and western United States and between the United States and Latin America, for instance, Boyd oversaw the building of four churches and one school in Panama.

Also in 1896, Boyd established and became secretary of the National Baptist Publishing Board in Nashville, Tennessee. Four years later, he moved his family to Nashville and oversaw the publication of the first Baptist literature for mass consumption. At Boyd's urging, the board also published literature for African American Baptist Sunday schools.

In large part because of Boyd's domination of the church's successful publishing firm, some leaders of the national church wanted to incorporate the National Baptist Convention and make it more of a business. Boyd led the fight against incorporation, and when the dust settled, he found himself the sole owner of the publishing company. Boyd's own books, a total of fourteen about the Baptist denomination, were published by his company.

♦ To **incorporate** is to gain certain legal advantages and recognition as a business in exchange for following certain rules.

Although Boyd did not want his church to become a business, he liked starting businesses. He even started businesses outside the

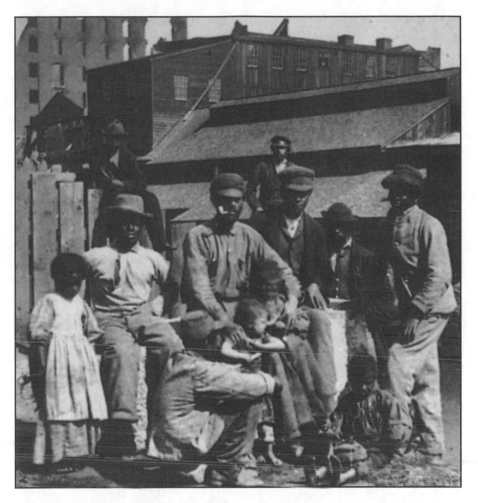

After the devastating Civil War, the newly emancipated slaves banded together to help each other face an uncertain future. (Library of Congress)

church. He was the founder in 1904 and first president of the One Cent Savings Bank and Trust Company (later renamed the Citizen's Savings Bank and Trust Company of Nashville). The following year, he and his son, Henry Allen Boyd, established the Nashville Globe Printing Company and the weekly African American newspaper, *Nashville Globe and Independent*.

Boyd also originated the idea of making black dolls for black children. His National Negro Doll Company was the first in the nation to make ethnic dolls.

Boyd died of a cerebral hemorrhage and stroke on August 19, 1922, at the age of seventy-nine. His son, Henry Allen Boyd, succeeded him as publisher and president of the *Globe and Independent* and took control of the publishing firm. He also ran his father's bank, which, unlike many other black-owned banks, managed to weather the Great Depression a decade later.

GRANVILLE T.
WOODS

(1856–1910)

✦

The quarter century that followed the Civil War was a great period of invention. Americans rushed to enter the machine age, harnessing energy to complicated devices with moving parts. Among them was Granville T. Woods, a prolific, enterprising inventor who did pioneering work in the field of electrical engineering.

Born in Columbus, Ohio, on April 23, 1856, Granville Woods was just five years old when the Civil War broke out. He attended school only until he was ten, then he went to work as an apprentice to learn machine repair and blacksmithing. Five years later, he left Ohio for Missouri, where he used the basic mechanical knowledge he had learned while serving his apprenticeship to get a job on the Iron Mountain Railroad. He served first as a fireman and then as an engineer.

When Woods discovered the new and growing field of electrical engineering, he began to read all he could on the subject. By the time he was twenty, he had saved enough money to enroll in night school to study mechanical and electrical engineering. But Woods was unable

to use his knowledge in either of those fields because no one would hire him.

In 1878, Woods obtained work as an engineer aboard a British steamer, *Ironsides,* and in 1880 took a job as an engineer on a steam locomotive on the D&S (Danville and Southern) Railroad.

Prevented from advancing in any of the jobs he worked, he turned his mechanical skills to invention. Woods's first patent, secured in June 1884 when he was twenty-eight years old, was for an improved steam boiler furnace. But his real interest was in solving some of the problems he had identified on the new electric railways.

Woods's second patent, for a telephone transmitter, was granted in December 1884. His first two patents were assigned to other individuals, indicating that he lacked the capital to market and manufacture them on his own. But in April of 1895, he patented an apparatus for transmission of messages by electricity, which combined features of both the telephone and the telegraph. Operators using this device could transmit messages either by Morse code or by voice. Woods was able to sell this invention to the Bell Telephone Company of Boston, and it was probably this sale that gave him the needed capital to establish his own company, Woods' Railway Telegraph Company, in Cincinnati.

In working on communications apparatus, Woods was trying to solve a problem that plagued the electric railways: the inability of the conventional telegraph to communicate between moving trains. Train collisions were common because engineers were unable to communicate with one another. Woods patented his Synchronous Multiplex Railway Telegraphy, which he marketed as being "for the purpose of averting accidents by keeping each train informed of the whereabouts of the one immediately ahead and following it; in communicating with stations from moving trains..."[1]

The Edison and Phelps Company, co-founded by Thomas Edison, had also been working on a railway telegraph, and the company contested Woods's claim to inventing the technology. But the patent office, in the case of *Woods* v. *Phelps*, twice declared Woods the inventor.

An article in the April 1, 1887, issue of the *American Catholic Tribune* called Woods "the greatest electrician in the world."

Woods reorganized his company as a manufacturing concern and called it Wood Electric Company. He continued to improve his idea for a new, more reliable communication system. Woods eventually sold more of his inventions to the American Bell Telephone Company.

In 1890, Woods moved to New York City, whose large electric railway system no doubt provided more opportunities for an electrical engineer. The 1895 *City Directory* lists "Granville T. Woods, electrician, 136 Liberty Street." There, joined from time to time by his brother, Lyates, who also had several inventions to his credit, Woods patented many improvements in the equipment used in the electric streetcar system. One of his more notable inventions was a grooved wheel that not only allowed the car to receive the electrical current but also reduced friction. Troller, the name given to this wheel, is the source of the popular name for streetcar—trolley car.

In 1902, Woods patented an automatic air brake, the rights to which were purchased by the Westinghouse Air Brake Company.

Among the many patents secured by Woods over the nearly twenty years of his greatest invention activity were those for an overhead conducting system for electric railways, an automatic safety cutout for electric circuits, a system of electric distribution, and a galvanic battery. Altogether, some sixty patents were registered in Woods's name, and by the time he died in 1910, he had become known as the "black Edison."

PART THREE

◆

INTO THE NEW CENTURY

MADAME C. J. WALKER

(1867–1919)

✦

Madame C. J. Walker was the first American woman, black or white, to earn a million dollars. It was an amazing feat. Born in poverty of ex-slave parents in Louisiana on December 23, 1867, Sarah McWilliams was orphaned at the age of seven, married at the age of fourteen, and widowed at the age of twenty, when her husband was killed by a lynch mob.

The sole support of her young daughter, Lelia, who had been born in 1885, Sarah decided to leave Louisiana, with its memories of loss and death, and to make a new life in St. Louis, Missouri. She supported herself and her daughter in St. Louis by taking in laundry, sometimes working fourteen hours a day. She was determined that her daughter would have a better life than she.

Not long after they had relocated to St. Louis, Sarah McWilliams noticed that her hair was coming out. At the time, most black women braided their hair tightly before they went to bed at night, so that in the morning it would be straighter and easier to comb. The braids pulled on the scalp and made the hair fall out. Sarah McWilliams was

not the only woman with this problem, but there were no hair-care products on the market that could correct it. She tried everything that was available, but without success, so she experimented on her own.

Sarah later told this story: One night she had a dream in which a black man appeared to her and shared a special recipe. Some of the ingredients were very exotic, such as a plant grown in Africa. But she sent for all the ingredients, mixed them up according to the formula the man had given her in the dream, and tried the mixture out on herself. New hair started to grow.

Sarah McWilliams would not reveal her secret, but she was happy to share the mixture with her friends. Seeing an opportunity, she began to sell her special "Hair Grower." But she still had to take in laundry to make ends meet and provide for her daughter.

Lelia McWilliams was attending Knoxville College, a private black college in Tennessee, when Sarah received word that a brother who lived in Denver, Colorado, had died, leaving a wife and daughters. Sarah decided to go to Denver to live with her relatives and help out. In Denver, she started her laundry business and also continued to sell her "Hair Grower."

Not long after she arrived in Denver, Sarah met and fell in love with C. J. Walker, a newspaperman. They soon married, and C. J. Walker used his knowledge of selling by mail order to help Sarah expand her business. It was at this time that Sarah took the professional name Madame C. J. Walker because she thought it sounded more authoritative and would be good for business. But she and her husband disagreed over how large the business should grow. C. J. Walker was not nearly as ambitious as his wife, and although Madame C. J. Walker kept that name for the rest of her life, the marriage eventually ended.

By the time Sarah's daughter, Lelia, who had also taken the last name Walker, graduated from Knoxville College in 1906, her mother had stopped taking in laundry and was devoting all her time to her

Lelia McWilliams used her college education to help her mother amass a fortune manufacturing and selling beauty products and services. (Library of Congress)

fast-growing business. She had developed new products. Most other companies that made hair-care products for blacks concentrated on making hair straighteners. Madame Walker wanted to make products that could help grow healthy hair. She found her own market niche.

She was certain that she could increase her business if she could travel around the country selling her products. She put Lelia in charge of the mail-order business in Denver and started traveling throughout the South and East. Madame Walker also put Lelia in charge of the day-to-day operations of her new college (see box) and returned to the road.

CORNERING THE MARKET

Madame Walker certainly must have thought of selling her hair care preparations through department stores and pharmacies. But those options were closed to a black woman in her day. Instead, she sold her products by giving lectures at women's clubs and churches, and by taking out advertisements in local black newspapers.

Aware that she could do only so much selling on her own, and convinced that more black women should go into business for themselves, Madame Walker recruited and trained scores of women to use and sell Walker products. Some set up beauty salons in their homes; others sold Walker products door-to-door. In 1908, Madame Walker and Lelia relocated to Pittsburgh, Pennsylvania, and founded Lelia College to teach the Walker System of hair care. By 1910, the Walker Company had trained some 5,000 female agents who sold Walker products in the United States and abroad.

Lelia, who had become an astute businesswoman in her own right, eventually moved to New York City to expand the Walker Company's East Coast operations. In New York City, she changed her name to A'Lelia, built a lavish town house (which contained a completely equipped beauty salon) on West 136th Street in Harlem, and held parties for wealthy and artistic people of all races.

Madame Walker, by now a millionaire, also relocated to New York. Several other American women were millionaires, but they had inherited their wealth, either from their families or from their husbands. Madame Walker was the first woman to earn her million from her own business. This was an astounding accomplishment for a black woman. To celebrate her success, she hired black architect Vertner Tandy to design and build a huge mansion for her on the Hudson River in upstate New York. She named it Villa Lewaro.

Sadly, Madame Walker was unable to enjoy her new mansion for long. The years of traveling and hard work had taken their toll, and she died of kidney failure resulting from hypertension in 1919, at the age of fifty.

In her will, she directed that the Walker Company always be headed by a woman, and her wishes were carried out. A'Lelia Walker headed the company and was succeeded by her daughter. The Walker Company continues to do business today.

Madame Walker, shown here leaving her home, was one of America's greatest business successes. She often toured the country seeking new customers. (Library of Congress)

Maggie Lena
WALKER

(1867–1934)

◆

When blacks could at last come together to develop economic resources in their own communities, the first thing they did was to look for ways to help themselves and one another. They established fraternal groups, or lodges, known as "burial aid societies," whose purpose was to provide support during health emergencies or deaths in their families. Group members paid monthly or weekly dues called premiums, and the money was kept in a general fund.

The first banks organized by African Americans grew out of such funds. One was the Capital Savings Bank, which opened its doors in Washington, D.C., in 1888. That same year, the Savings Bank of the Grand Foundation of the United Order of True Believers was organized in Richmond, Virginia.

The first African American woman to become president of a bank was born in deep poverty in Richmond, on July 15, 1867. Maggie Lena Walker, who was not related to Madame C. J. Walker, was the older of William and Elizabeth Mitchell's two children. Elizabeth had been born a slave, and William worked as a cook and a butler.

Maggie Lena grew up with confidence in herself and in her community. As a senior at Armstrong Normal School in Richmond, she was part of a protest against segregated commencement exercises that historians believe was the first school strike of blacks in the United States.

Upon graduation, the teenage Maggie Lena Mitchell taught at the Lancaster School. In 1890, she married Armistead Walker, who worked in his father's bricklaying and construction business. The couple would have three sons and adopt a daughter.

In 1890, Maggie Lena Walker also became secretary for the Order of St. Luke, a burial aid society. At the time, the Order of St. Luke had 3,408 members but no funds of any consequence, no property, and virtually no staff.

With her usual confidence, Maggie Lena Walker determined to build up the business by increasing membership and by wisely investing the members' dues money so that it would grow. In 1902, she founded the *St. Luke Herald*, a newspaper that kept the membership informed of local events and the operations and activities of the business. That same year, she proposed the St. Luke Penny Savings Bank. The members liked her idea. So the bank opened its doors in 1903 with Walker as its president, the first black woman bank president in America.

> ✦ You are **investing** when you buy all or part of something that you expect to become even more valuable later on.
>
> ✦ Your **assets** include all of the things that you own.
>
> ✦ **Merge** means to join. In a **merger** two businesses join together to become one.

Walker concentrated on helping young people and adults with little income. She established an educational loan fund, granted mortgages to people who had been turned down by white-owned banks, and managed to build the bank's assets steadily. Within twenty-five years, she had increased the bank's clientele to over 100,000.

In 1904, Walker introduced a Supply Department for the Order of

THE TRAILBLAZER

In a book called *Sister Power*, author Patricia Reid Merritt tells the story of Emma Chappell, an entrepreneur who is following in Maggie Lena Walker's footsteps today:

"After working thirty years at Continental Bank, one of the largest banks in the city of Philadelphia, Emma was ready to start a bank of her own. With the support of black ministers she raised the start-up money from the people in local churches. She came up with $6 million to open United Bank. Emma paid back their trust with personal loans, business loans, and housing loans. High school kids came to learn how to plan and start their own businesses. Neighborhood groups learned how to make investments. After only two years, she would expand United to five branches and $100 million in deposits."

St. Luke, which eventually grew into a three-floor department store on East Broad Street, the main business street in Richmond. Although the enterprise later failed, it showed Walker's entrepreneurial thinking.

In 1929, the St. Luke Bank merged with other African American banks in Richmond to become the Consolidated Bank and Trust Company. As its leader, Walker oversaw construction of a $100,000 headquarters for the bank and increased its staff to 55 full-time employees. Throughout Virginia and the surrounding states, 145 field-workers provided excellent service to the members of the Order of St. Luke.

As Walker built the business, she also built her own reputation. She inspired 1,400 women to raise the money to build a home for delinquent black girls in Richmond. She also headed an interracial group of women who built a community center for the city. In 1930, when the well-known educator Mary McLeod Bethune formed a new black women's organization, the National Council of Negro Women,

Maggie Lena Walker was among those present at the very first meeting.

Maggie Lena Walker died on December 15, 1934, at the age of sixty-seven. In 1978, the row house at 110½ East Leigh Street in Richmond, which had been her home, was placed on the list of National Historic Sites.

CHARLES CLINTON
SPAULDING

(1874–1952)

✦

Charles Clinton Spaulding also found opportunities in the burgeoning black self-help movement that followed Emancipation. He was born on August 1, 1874, on a farm in Columbus County, North Carolina, in a close-knit community of free blacks who had settled there in the early nineteenth century. He was one of fourteen children of Margaret Ann Moore Spaulding and Benjamin McIver Spaulding, a hardworking farmer who also made furniture, worked as a blacksmith, and served as county sheriff.

Charles, the second son of ten surviving children, worked on his father's farm and attended the local school whenever his farm work permitted. By the time he turned twenty, he knew that he wanted more from life than farming could provide, and he moved to Durham, North Carolina, to stay with his uncle, Dr. Aaron McDuffie Moore, the first black doctor in the city.

Spaulding attended high school in Durham, all the while working at various jobs, including dishwasher, bellhop, waiter, and office boy for a white attorney. Like the other great entrepreneurs in this

collection, he thrived on hard work. On graduation, he got a job as a clerk in a cooperative grocery store established by local blacks. He was soon appointed manager of the store, and he worked hard to make it successful, despite lack of interest on the part of the original investors. Eventually, he found himself running the business alone.

In 1898, his uncle, Dr. Moore, along with John Merrick, the city's leading barber, and five others, founded the North Carolina Mutual and Provident Association. Charles Spaulding sold life insurance policies for the company while he headed the grocery cooperative. In 1900, Merrick and Moore reorganized the association and hired Spaulding as general manager. That year, Spaulding also married Fannie Jones, and they eventually had three sons and a daughter.

Spaulding dedicated himself to building the business and helping it to prosper. He recruited part-time agents to sell policies, and by 1902, there were agents in fifty towns throughout the state. He started a monthly company newspaper and advertised extensively, putting the North Carolina Mutual name on calendars, medical thermometers, and many other items useful to consumers. By 1903, more than 100,000 policyholders were enrolled with the company. And by 1908, the company had purchased lots near its headquarters and built a complex for black businesses, which included a barber shop operated by John Merrick, a drugstore, a tailor, and a newspaper.

Two important people in Spaulding's life died in 1919: his wife, Fannie, and John Merrick. Spaulding married Charlotte Stevens Gardner the following year and oversaw the reorganization of the enterprise into a full-service insurance company, North Carolina Mutual Life Insurance Company. In 1923, on the death of Dr. Moore, Spaulding became president of North Carolina Mutual, which he worked to build into the world's largest all-black enterprise.

North Carolina Mutual eventually included banks, a real estate company, and a mortgage company. Spaulding became the most

Digging Out of the Great Depression

When the Great Depression descended on the nation after the stock market crash of 1929, Spaulding was one of the leaders who helped to provide relief from its hardships. Millions of people all over the country had lost their jobs, their savings, and their homes. By 1933, 16 million people—one third of the labor force—were unemployed. Spaulding worked to inform blacks of government efforts to provide relief, to receive complaints of violations against blacks, and to support President Franklin Delano Roosevelt's New Deal employment programs.

Also during the depression, Spaulding helped to win back the vote that Southern blacks had lost after Reconstruction. He led a committee of the Durham Council on Negro Affairs, which eventually registered thousands of black voters.

powerful black in Durham and one of the most influential in the nation, endorsing political candidates and mounting campaigns to save such venerable black institutions as Shaw University in Raleigh, North Carolina, Virginia Theological Seminary, and the National Negro Business League.

Although he privately supported the efforts of the National Association for the Advancement of Colored People (NAACP) to legally challenge segregation, Spaulding shunned publicity and would cease his support if it were ever discovered. He believed in the system that had brought him success, and during World War II he worked tirelessly for black support for the war effort. He invested nearly $405 million dollars of Mutual's funds in war bonds.

Spaulding died of heart failure on August 1, 1952, his seventy-eighth birthday. His funeral was the largest in Durham's history, and the mayor of the city proclaimed a day of respect to Spaulding's memory. Although people thought that Spaulding was a millionaire, he was in fact *not* one. He was always an employee, never an owner, of North Carolina Mutual, the company to which he devoted his skills. North Carolina Mutual remains today the nation's largest black insurance enterprise, and Spaulding's descendants are among the nation's most successful entrepreneurs.

PHILIP A. PAYTON JR.

(1876–1917)

✦

One of the marks of an entrepreneur is the ability to identify a need and to figure out how to fill it. Philip A. Payton Jr. saw that black New Yorkers in the early twentieth century needed decent housing, and he found it for them—in a part of the city called Harlem, where grand, new apartment buildings stood empty on broad, tree-lined avenues.

Payton was born on February 27, 1876, in Westfield, Massachusetts, and he grew up there, close to country life. He graduated from Livingston College in Salisbury, North Carolina, in 1898, and in 1899, he moved to New York City, determined to make his fortune. Although he was college educated, the jobs available to young black men did not require a college degree. He worked as a barber, as a slot machine attendant in a department store, and as a porter in an apartment building before he saw his opportunity to become an entrepreneur and work for himself.

Realizing that black newcomers like himself needed real estate agents in the city, Payton decided to become the first. But his early

attempts were failures. As he recalled, "Besides being dispossessed three times and once evicted for non-payment of rent, I have walked from Nassau Street to Harlem on more than one occasion for want of a nickel."[1]

According to an article in the New York *Tribune* of July 26, 1904, it was an instance of outright discrimination against blacks that elevated Payton to fame in Harlem real estate as the founder of the Afro-American Realty Company in 1904: "The corporation got its start about a year ago in the attempt of one of the well known realty companies of this city to oust the negro tenants of One-hundred-and-thirty-fifth Street between Fifth and Lenox Avenues, the object being to make it a 'white' street and raise rentals. Wealthy negroes who were interested in real estate resented this attempt, got together, and after vainly trying to get leaseholds on property in that street, bought outright two flat [apartment] houses tenanted by whites, dispossessed them and rented the flats to negroes who had been put out of the other houses."[2]

The Afro-American Realty Company was a partnership among Payton and some of the most prominent black businessmen in New York: James C. Thomas, an undertaker, James C. Garner, whose business was house cleaning and renovating; Willard H. Smith, an attorney; Fred R. Moore, a journalist; William H. Brooks, a clergyman; and Charles W. Anderson, the city's leading Republican politician.

The company would acquire five-year leases on Harlem property owned by whites and then rent to black tenants. In some cases, it evicted white tenants in order to rent to blacks—whom, according to critics, it charged higher rents than the white tenants. But the need for decent housing by African American New Yorkers was so great that they were willing to pay almost anything. The Afro-American Realty Company opened up more and more previously all-white buildings to blacks, earning Payton the nickname "Father of [Black] Harlem."

A LUCKY BREAK...

It may have been on one of his walks to Harlem, far north of the central city, that Payton seized upon his big idea. The black sections on the West Side of Manhattan were overpopulated and squalid, whereas the large, new apartment buildings in Harlem were practically empty. Before the early 1900s, Harlem was a predominantly white community that was expected to become a well-to-do residential area connected to the center of New York City by new subway and rail lines. But real estate developers overextended themselves in their rush to prepare for the coming of the white tenants who never arrived.

Payton established a real estate business in Harlem and advertised "Management of Colored Tenements a Specialty." At first he was rebuffed by the white landlords who controlled Harlem's apartment buildings. No one wanted to rent to blacks. But circumstances soon forced them to do so.

Payton's opportunity came when two landlords of adjoining houses in Harlem got into a dispute, and one of them, to spite his enemy, turned his building over to Payton to fill with black tenants. Seeing Payton's success, other Harlem landlords approached him about renting their apartments.

In 1906, forty-three of the company's stockholders sued Payton for fraud and embezzlement. But the suit was dismissed because Payton was only one of several officers in the company. Nevertheless, the company was beset by financial irregularities, and the lawsuit, together with several unsuccessful speculations, forced the company to cease operations in 1908.

Other black realtors established themselves in Harlem. Nail and Parker, owned by John E. Nail and Henry C. Parker, became the largest and most successful black-owned real estate operation in the district.

Payton continued in the real estate business on his own, managing buildings from his home in Harlem. He died in Harlem on August 29, 1917.

OSCAR
MICHEAUX

(1884–1951)

✦

Like Philip Payton, Oscar Micheaux identified a need—for movies with black actors and actresses to entertain black audiences. He also proved that a black star system could exist.

Born on January 2, 1884, in Metropolis, Illinois, Micheaux was one of thirteen children. His parents had been slaves, but he managed to acquire an education. Apparently, it was his income from working as a Pullman car porter that enabled him to buy two 160-acre tracts of land in South Dakota, where he established a homestead.

Then Micheaux's life took an artistic turn. He wrote *The Conquest: The Story of a Negro Pioneer*, a novel based on his experiences as a homesteader. Micheaux published the novel himself in 1913 and established the Western Book Supply Company to market it. From then on, his business ventures all fit together. His experiences as a bookseller became the basis for his second novel, *The Forged Note: A Romance of the Darker Races*. His third novel, *The Homesteader*, published in 1917, attracted the attention of a movie producer, George P. Johnson.

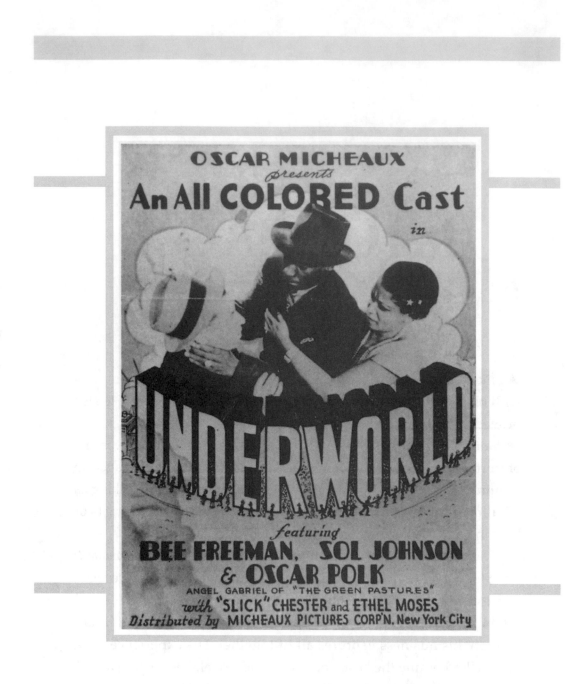

George Johnson and his brother, Noble, an actor, owned the Lincoln Film Company, which had offices in Los Angeles, California, and Omaha, Nebraska. They were among the pioneers in the new field of filmmaking.

The Johnson brothers wanted to buy the film rights to Micheaux's novel, *The Homesteader*. Micheaux, who had become interested in filmmaking himself, agreed on condition that they allow him to direct the motion picture. The Johnsons refused. Micheaux decided to produce and direct the film himself, and he established the Micheaux Book and Film Company.

In 1919, just four years after the release of *Birth of a Nation* (see box on next page), Micheaux produced his first two films, *The Homesteader* and *Within Our Gates*.

Within Our Gates was set in the South after the Civil War, when most former slaves lived in virtual slavery as sharecroppers on white-owned farms. This film about white exploitation of black labor was so potentially explosive that both black and white church leaders in Chicago tried to cancel its showing, fearing that it would reignite the race riots that had recently plagued that city. Far from being worried about the controversy, Micheaux saw its potential for publicity. He drummed up attention in other cities by referring to the controversy and by advertising the "complete version" of the film.

Middle-class blacks did not support Micheaux, because they felt that he should have done more to uplift the race. But Micheaux was a born promoter. He would tour the country to publicize one film, carrying the prints from town to town, often for one-night stands, and use the opportunities presented along the way to raise money for his next film.

+ **Technology** refers to the scientific aspect of practical activities, such as making movies.

+ **Promotion** is the activity of getting people excited about buying something. The person who stirs things up is called the **promoter**.

+ A business is **bankrupt** when it can no longer pay its bills and has used up all its resources.

Birth of an Industry

The technology necessary to make moving pictures, although not the soundtrack to accompany the images, was pioneered in the early 1900s. Black themes in films appeared very early. For example, the 1903 *Uncle Tom's Cabin*, based on the Harriet Beecher Stowe novel, was about southern slaves escaping to freedom in the North and in Canada. The film's black characters were very sympathetic, and there was great melodrama in the scene in which a fugitive slave mother and her small child are caught on an ice floe.

But twelve years later, D.W. Griffith produced a film in which the image of blacks was radically different from that in *Uncle Tom's Cabin*. His 1915 *Birth of a Nation* is regarded even today as a landmark in filmmaking for its advanced (for the time) techniques. But in Griffith's story of the Reconstruction South in the grip of federal troops after the Confederate defeat in the Civil War, he brought to the large screen all the negative stereotypes in the nation's consciousness—marauding black soldiers and power-mad mulattoes (played by white actors in blackface makeup) threatening a white southern family that is eventually rescued by the Ku Klux Klan.

Birth of a Nation caused an uproar among black Americans. The National Association for the Advancement of Colored People organized a formal protest. And individual blacks determined to make films about black America in which positive images would counteract those of Griffith. Their films were called "race movies," and some 350 were produced between 1912 and 1948 by 150 companies; Oscar Micheaux accounted for 10 percent of those productions.

Micheaux was especially good at persuading the white owners and managers of segregated southern theaters to show his films at special matinee performances for blacks or at special late shows for whites.

His 1924 film *Body and Soul* starred Paul Robeson, who would go on to become the most famous African American actor and singer, until the 1960s when Sidney Poitier appeared in films.

Micheaux continued to make films throughout the 1920s and

Segregation was about keeping African Americans "in their place" in society. In segregated southern movie theaters where Oscar Micheaux ran his films, blacks had to sit in the balconies. (Schomburg Center for Research in Black Culture)

1930s, although his company went bankrupt in 1928 and the Great Depression made it difficult for anyone to stay in business. In the early 1930s, he successfully made the switch to "talkies," films with a soundtrack.

Oscar Micheaux died during a promotional tour in Charlotte, North Carolina, in 1951. By that time, major Hollywood studios had started making films with black casts, choking off the same independent black producers and distributors who had proved it was possible in the first place. Micheaux was generally forgotten, and most of his films were lost or destroyed. But historians now regard him as one of the most important figures in the development of cinema.

A. G.
GASTON

(1892–1996)

✦

Arthur George Gaston amassed a fortune estimated at between $30 million and $40 million by quietly and continually starting one business after another.

Gaston was born the grandson of a slave on July 4, 1892, in Demopolis, Alabama. When Arthur was a boy, his father died and his mother went to Birmingham to work in the homes of white people. Arthur stayed in Demopolis with his grandmother. Like most of the rest of the South, Demopolis was deeply segregated. Later in life, Gaston recalled that in his hometown "there wasn't much to inspire a black boy, but somehow I found the inspiration I needed."

There was a swing in his grandmother's backyard, and all the neighborhood kids used to go there to play on it. Seeing how popular the swing was, young Arthur founded the "first Gaston business" by charging the kids a pin or a button for the privilege of swinging. Once Arthur had filled a cigar box with buttons and pins, he sold them to women in the community who needed pins and buttons for their sewing.

On leaving high school (blacks in Demopolis could only attend through the tenth grade at that time), Gaston joined his mother in Birmingham and enrolled at Tuggle Institute, a trade school for blacks in the city. After graduating from Tuggle Institute, he worked as a laborer until the United States entered World War I in 1917. Gaston enlisted in the army, where he also worked as a laborer because blacks were not allowed to serve in combat.

After Gaston's discharge from the army, he returned to Birmingham and got a job at Tennessee Coal, Iron, and Steel Company. His job was to do odd tasks—digging holes, painting boxcars. He earned thirty-one cents an hour and worked ten and a half hours a day. But he had bigger plans.

+ A **budget** is the amount of money you have to spend and your plan for spending it.

+ **Interest** is the amount of money it costs to borrow more money, usually a percentage of the amount borrowed.

+ **Profit** is the money you make after you have paid all of your expenses.

First, he needed to save money. Gaston put himself on a tight budget. He would allow himself to spend only $10 a pay period (every two weeks): $5 for living expenses, such as food, and $5 for social activities, such as dating. But he soon earned a reputation for being cheap, and girls didn't want to go out with him. Philosophically, Gaston decided that this just meant he could save more. Then he met and married a girl named Creola Smith, who understood his dreams of the future.

In later life, Gaston said that the secret to becoming a businessman was to "start somewhere." With part of his savings, he began buying peanuts and selling them for a profit to his fellow workers. After he had saved enough money to lend some of it out, he started a loan business, charging interest of twenty-five cents on the dollar.

He did so well that in 1923 he started a burial aid society with his father-in-law, A. L. Smith. Gaston and Smith collected the payments and invested them, earning a profit for themselves while making good

MARTIN LUTHER KING'S FRIEND

After the civil rights movement began in the South, Gaston allowed Dr. Martin Luther King Jr. and other civil rights organizers, who were in Birmingham to plan a march, to meet in one of his motels. When King and his aide, the Reverend Ralph David Abernathy, were jailed for marching without a permit in Birmingham, Gaston personally posted the $5,000 bail, handing a check to the judge, who accepted it without question. Shortly afterward, Gaston's motel was damaged in a firebombing. The following September, his home was also a target. Two years later, in March 1965, Gaston offered a farm he owned as a rest station for marchers on the famous Selma-to-Montgomery march for voting rights. It was a sad note that Martin Luther King Jr. was assassinated on April 4, 1968, while staying at Gaston's Lorraine Motel in Memphis, Tennessee.

Although Gaston supported the civil rights movement, he believed that what black people needed was "a Martin Luther King of economics who will fire the people up like they are being fired up for civil rights." He went on to say, "It doesn't do any good to arrive at first-class citizenship if you arrive broke."[1]

on their agreements to provide proper burial for their customers. They soon expanded their business to an insurance company. Reinvesting their profits, they started a funeral home, which eventually grew into a chain of fourteen across Alabama.

As the businesses grew, Gaston had difficulty finding enough black clerks and typists to work for him. So he started the Booker T. Washington Business College to train them. Realizing that it was hard for blacks to get financing to buy homes of their own, he founded the Citizens Federal Savings and Loan Association.

The majority of the businesses Gaston founded were not intended to make a huge profit. All he wanted was to live comfortably and, whenever possible, to fill a need he had identified among black people. There was just one time when he went into a business purely to make money, and he lived to regret it. In the late 1930s, the famous black heavyweight boxing champion Joe Louis started a soft drink business called Joe Louis Punch. Thinking he could make "a killing," Gaston invested in a Joe Louis Punch franchise. He also started his own Brown Belle Bottling Company, investing heavily in the necessary machinery. Joe Louis Punch proved not to be as popular as the boxer, and the company went out of business.

As the years went by, Gaston went into a variety of other businesses, including radio stations and motels. His personal fortune was in the tens of millions. But he never forgot where he had come from, and he kept on his office wall a tinted photograph of himself as a seven-year-old, standing by an oxcart in front of an unpainted cabin.

Arthur George Gaston died in January 1996, at the age of 103.

ADA "BRICKTOP"
SMITH

(1894–1984)

✦

Anyone given the name Ada Beatrice Queen Victoria Louise Virginia Smith at birth was destined for greatness. But it was by the simple nickname "Bricktop" that a small black woman from Alderson, West Virginia, became known internationally as a nightclub owner.

Bricktop was born on August 14, 1894, the youngest of four children and the only one with red hair. Her father, Thomas Smith, a barber, died when she was four. Her mother, Hattie E. Smith, who was of mixed Irish and African heritage, had been born in slavery. After Thomas Smith's death, the family moved to Chicago.

Bricktop attended an integrated public school on Chicago's South Side, but school did not interest her. What fascinated her was the music and dancing that seemed to fill the streets of her neighborhood. She was tiny when she first began to peek under the doors of local saloons and yearn to be part of the happy atmosphere. Bricktop loved to go to Saturday matinees at the Pekin Theatre, which featured black entertainment. She was only sixteen when she quit school and joined

the chorus that was touring with Miller and Lyles, a popular black comedy and musical team.

Bricktop finally got a chance to perform as a singer at Chicago clubs, including one owned by Jack Johnson, the famous black heavyweight boxer. In 1922, she relocated to New York, where the nightclub business was also thriving.

Arriving in Paris in 1924 to sing in a small club called Le Grand Duc, Bricktop was soon discovered by American composer Cole Porter, who had a home in the city. He brought his friends, who included American millionaires, European royalty, and international stars, to Le Grand Duc, and soon Bricktop had taken over management of the club, which was renamed Bricktop's. The business grew, not so much because of her singing or her willingness to give lessons in the latest American jazz dances, but because of her ability to make her patrons feel that Bricktop's was a "home away from home."

The stock market crash in New York in 1929 was felt as far away as Europe, and Bricktop watched as the numbers of wealthy guests dwindled. But she managed to keep Bricktop's going until the onset of

THE "IN" PLACE TO GO

The black section of Manhattan called Harlem had become the "in" place to go for music and drink, for in the years after World War I, the music, art, and literature of blacks were suddenly all the rage. African American artists and writers were inspired by Harlem's busy streets and special style. The era of the Harlem Renaissance had begun.

A similar interest in both African American and African culture was developing in Europe, largely because of the exposure of Europeans to these cultures during World War I. When Bricktop learned that opportunities for black American entertainers existed in Paris, she was quick to take advantage.

World War II. As Adolf Hitler's Nazi troops threatened Paris, all Americans were warned to flee. Bricktop, with the aid of the Duchess of Windsor, set sail for the United States on one of the last ships to leave France before German occupation.

In New York, Bricktop was unable to duplicate her Paris success, but she relocated to Mexico City, where she ran successful clubs until the war was over. In 1951, she moved to Rome. She operated a succession of clubs there, playing host to the American film stars who had become the new royalty, although she never quite accepted them as equal to her clientele in her golden years in Paris.

✦ **Clientele** is another word for customers or patrons.

In semi-retirement for the last few years of her life because of ill health, she died in 1984 at the age of eighty-nine—just a few months after her autobiography, *Bricktop*, was published.

JAKE
SIMMONS JR.

(1901–1981)

✦

Some blacks in Texas and Oklahoma found themselves in a unique position in the early twentieth century—oil had been discovered on their land. Many sold their oil rights for very little money, but Jake Simmons figured out what oil rights were really worth and made a fortune.

Simmons was born on January 17, 1901, in Muskogee County, Oklahoma, which at the time was part of United States Indian Territory. His grandfather, Cow Tom, had been brought to the area as a slave to the Creek Indians in 1837 and had risen to become one of the few black chiefs of an Indian tribe. Nowhere else in the United States were blacks able to live in such dignity as they did in the Creek nation. When Jake Jr. was born, Muskogee was predominantly black, and it had black elected officials.

Jake's mother, Rose Jefferson, was Cow Tom's daughter. Proud and educated, she married Jake Sr., an illiterate but hard-working rancher who had been born in a Confederate refugee camp during the Civil War and whose mother was half Creek and half black. The

ninth child of Rose Jefferson and Jake Sr., Jake Jr. grew up on the family ranch. He was still a child when he, like other members of his family, received a 160-acre "freehold" from the United States government. At the urging of white settlers who wanted Oklahoma to become a state, the federal government had dissolved the Creek government and allotted each member of the tribe 160 acres.

By the time he was ten years old, Jake Jr. was an excellent rider, and he trained his father's racing horses. But he had decided that ranching was not to his taste. In 1914, he was sent to Tuskegee Institute to be educated, and while there, he discovered the entrepreneurial drive of Tuskegee's founder, Booker T. Washington.

While at Tuskegee, Simmons was secretly married to a classmate, Melba Dorsey, to whom a daughter was born the following year. Melba was from Detroit, and the couple settled there. Simmons went to work as a machinist in a Packard automobile factory. He invented a windshield defroster that caused engine exhaust to disappear, and he secured a patent for it. But his superiors paid no attention, not believing that a black man could invent anything useful.

Jake Simmons Jr. just decided he was not cut out to work for anyone but himself. Unhappy in the North, and faced with an ultimatum from his father either to divorce Melba or be disowned, he obeyed his father and returned home. In 1920, he married Eva Flowers, a girl from Muskogee.

The oil boom in Oklahoma and Texas was in full swing by the time Simmons married for a second time, and he grasped the opportunities immediately. He began to broker, or act as a middleman, between blacks and Indians and white oilmen. He made sure that the landowners got a good price, and in return, he got a percentage of that price for himself.

✦ A **broker** is the person who acts as a middleman to bring people together who want to do business.

Over time, Simmons became very influential in Muskogee, but when he ran for political office, he failed each time, a victim of increasing hostility to blacks in power in government. He found that he was much more successful in using his influence behind the scenes to work for white candidates who he felt would treat blacks and Indians fairly.

By the 1960s, when many African nations gained their independence, Simmons saw another opportunity for himself in the oil-rich nations of Nigeria and Ghana. He introduced West African nations seeking outside investment to international American mineral companies looking for opportunities in foreign lands. As an agent for the mammoth Phillips Petroleum oil company, he paved the way for Ghana's oil industry. In 1978, he was awarded Ghana's Grand Medal.

Simmons died on March 25, 1981, a millionaire many times over. His son Donald had been groomed to take over his international business and runs it today.

JANET HARMON
BRAGG

(1907–1993)

◆

Janet Harmon Bragg, probably the first African American woman to own an airplane, was born in Griffin, Georgia, not quite thirty miles from Atlanta. She was the youngest of seven children born to Samuel Harmon, a brick contractor, and Cordia Butts Harmon, a homemaker. Somehow, her parents managed to feed, clothe, and educate all seven of their children and to teach their three daughters that "if Jack can do it, so can Jill."[1]

Janet earned a degree in nursing from Spelman Seminary (later Spelman College), a school for African American women in Atlanta. Her first job was at the hospital in her hometown. She stayed only a month, however, shocked by two separate incidents in which patients in the small black section of the hospital died because they had received inadequate treatment. Aware that the situation would be the same at hospitals elsewhere in the South, she joined relatives in Chicago.

But the North proved to be as segregated in its own way as the South. Bragg was unsuccessful at first in finding a nursing job. She

cleaned bathrooms in a large Chicago hotel, worked briefly in a lamp-shade factory, and did private-duty nursing before finally managing to land a job as night supervisor in the emergency room of Wilson Hospital. She also studied laboratory procedures and radiology at nearby Chicago Medical School. During that time, she met and married her first husband, Evans Waterford.

The marriage ended after two years. Around the same time, Bragg's father died, and her mother and two nieces moved to Chicago to live with her. Bragg needed to make more money, so she went to work as a health inspector for the Metropolitan Burial Assurance Association. The increased income enabled her not only to care for her family but also to pursue her avocation, flying.

Chicago was the home of black aviation, thanks to the Curtiss Wright Flying Service, which admitted African Americans. Two of its black graduates taught ground school classes to blacks. Janet Bragg was the first woman in the class, which eventually numbered twenty-seven students, including six women, although all but Bragg and Willa Brown eventually dropped out. Students learned meteorology, aerodynamics, airplane mechanics, and aircraft maintenance.

The members of the class were so enthusiastic about flying that they formed the Challenger Aero Club. Blacks were banned from most white airports, so they built their own airfield in Robbins, Illinois, an all-black community south of Chicago. Bragg used her savings to buy the club's first plane, a used Curtiss OX-5, for which she paid about $500.

Bragg earned her first pilot's license in 1932 and passed the test for a private pilot's license two years later. She soon bought a brand-new Piper Cub airplane, which she rented to the Aero Club.

Bragg became an entrepreneur quite by accident. Her brother backed out of a deal they had made to buy a two-apartment house in Chicago. A friend who was a nursing-home supervisor suggested that she turn the building into a home for recovering patients who were on

A Tenacious Spirit

After World War II broke out in Europe and the United States began to prepare for war, Bragg applied first to the WASPS, the Women's Auxiliary Service Pilots, and then to the military nurses corps. She was turned down by both because of her race. Still determined, she decided to obtain her commercial flying certificate. She took the required classes at the newly established first training school for black pilots at Tuskegee Institute in Alabama.

When the time came to take the test, she flawlessly executed the maneuvers required in the flying part of the test. But the federal flight examiner from Birmingham told the Tuskegee instructors, "I will put her up against any of your flight instructors. But I've never given a colored girl a commercial license, and I don't intend to now."[2] Bragg had to return to Chicago to take the flight test, which she passed. She was awarded her commercial pilot's license in 1942.

Bragg never got to use her commercial pilot's license to earn a living, because opportunities for black commercial pilots were almost nonexistent. But the same tenacious spirit she showed in securing that license brought her success later in another field of endeavor.

welfare. The city of Chicago paid for the patients' housing, and Bragg's first rent check, $800, was the most money she'd ever had at one time.

Because her cousins from Georgia helped out at the nursing home, Bragg was able to keep her job at Metropolitan. Only after she married Sumner Bragg, a supervisor at Metropolitan, in 1951, did she resign from the company. Two years later, she purchased a twenty-two-room mansion and expanded her nursing-home business. The Braggs eventually bought the slightly smaller mansion next door, and were able to care for sixty patients.

Over the years, the Harmon-Bragg nursing home housed more than convalescents. The ballroom of the larger mansion often served as a dormitory for students from Ethiopia. During World War II, John Robinson, one of Bragg's first flight instructors, had gone to Ethiopia to establish its air force. In 1955, because of her aid to the students, Bragg spent three months in Ethiopia as the official guest of Emperor Haile Selassie.

Janet Bragg died in 1993. Her autobiography was appropriately titled *Soaring Above Setbacks*.

PART FOUR

MODERN TIMES

HENRY G.
PARKS
(1916–1989)

✦

Catering and food services have always been areas in which blacks could prosper, if they had the chance. Henry G. Parks took the opportunities he found to build one of the largest black food companies in the United States.

Parks was born in Atlanta, Georgia, on September 20, 1916, to poor parents who both worked as domestics. World War I broke out the following year, and the expanding northern war industries were a magnet for southern blacks looking for jobs. The Parks family joined the northward migration, settling in Dayton, Ohio. Henry Parks attended public schools in Dayton and then enrolled at Ohio State University. He graduated with a bachelor of science degree and then did special studies in marketing.

Henry Parks's dream was to own a business, but many believed that was a nearly impossible goal for a black man in the United States in the 1930s. A counselor at Ohio State University told Parks that if he wanted to be a success in business, he should do two things: change his name, and go to South America to acquire a Spanish accent.

- ✦ **Marketing** is the part of running a business that focuses on selling the product and getting people to want to buy it.

- ✦ **Financing** is the part of running a business that attends to finding the money to pay the expenses.

- ✦ **Production** is the part of running a business that sees to making products that work and to making them on time and for the right price.

- ✦ **Distribution** is the part of a business that concerns getting the product to the customer.

- ✦ Having **stock** in a company means that you own part of the company.

The counselor believed that Parks would be much better off pretending to be a Latino businessman than an African American one. But Parks replied that he would not run from anything, least of all himself.

Parks set out to prove the doubters wrong. Eventually, he moved to New York where he owned and operated several businesses, including a theatrical booking agency. Like A. G. Gaston, he also attempted to form a soft drink company with the great black boxing champion Joe Louis. But the product, Joe Louis Punch, failed to catch on. Parks relocated to Baltimore, where at various times he owned a drugstore, dealt in real estate, and ran a cement block plant. Unfortunately, each effort failed.

Then his luck changed. In 1951, believing that there was a market for southern-style sausage in Baltimore's black community, he and several others founded Parks Sausage Company. They took an old Virginia recipe, adapted it to make huge amounts, and set up a plant and their offices in a rented building. Six people did all the work of the company. Parks was the company's chief marketer.

Henry Parks understood that a successful business has certain features, including a reputation for quality and good employer-employee relations. Parks did not wait for problems to arise. Instead, he invited federal meat inspectors into his plants from the start. Even before coding became law, he coded his products to indicate when they should no longer be sold. Parks also welcomed the labor unions in before they approached him.

In 1969, Parks Sausage Company became the first black-owned business to offer its stock to the public. Within two years, Parks Sausage Company had contracts with every major East Coast supermarket chain, a total of 12,000 stores, 75 percent of which were in white suburbs. In 1971, the company's sales reached $10.4 million.

Millions of Americans knew of Parks sausage through a memorable advertisement in which a little boy calls, "More Parks sausages, Mom…pleeeease?" Very few realized that the company was owned by blacks.

Henry G. Parks died in 1989, just as the sausage business in general went into a slump. Perhaps the factory was too large or the company's debt was too difficult to handle. Baltimore's largest black-owned business closed its doors on May 24, 1996, and filed for bankruptcy.

Many people were disappointed that such a great black success story had reached an unhappy end. Franco Harris, former running back for the Pittsburgh Steelers football team, was one of those

THE MARKETER

Although the fledgling Parks Sausage Company had every problem associated with starting a new business—from financing to production, to obtaining raw materials to distribution—Parks's studies in marketing paid off. Knowing that the church was the heart of any black community, he sponsored breakfasts for ministers. He also hired a barker to dress as "Parky the Pig" and parade through town handing out free sausages. He hired saleswomen to promote the product in beauty shops and salesmen to go to barber shops and shoeshine stands. Parks sausages soon caught on in Baltimore, and Henry Parks then set his sights on the black community in Washington, D.C. There, he signed up the first supermarket chain to sell his sausages.

businesspeople determined to rescue the company and all it had stood for in the black community. He had a company of his own, Super Bakery Inc. of Pittsburgh. In June 1996, it was announced that Harris's company would purchase H. G. Parks, Inc. Perhaps there is new life yet for Henry G. Parks's dream.

JOHN H.
JOHNSON

(B. 1918)

✦

John H. Johnson made his fortune as a magazine publisher in Chicago, which became a mecca for southern blacks in the early years of this century. He was born January 19, 1918, in the little town of Arkansas City, Arkansas. His father, Leroy Johnson, a laborer, was killed in a sawmill accident when John was eight years old. The following year, his mother, Gertrude Jenkins Johnson, married James Williams, who delivered groceries for a bakery.

Life was hard, and everyone in the family had to work. According to Johnson, "I was a working child. I learned how to work before I learned how to play."[1] Nevertheless, his mother insisted that he attend school, which he did through eighth grade. There was no high school for blacks in Arkansas City. In order to make enough money to go to Chicago, where he could attend high school, Johnson helped his mother do laundry and cook for camps of levee workers. He became a master cook in the process.

Johnson was fifteen years old in 1933, when he had at last saved enough money to go to Chicago. Although his mother had to be

separated for a time from her husband, whom she loved dearly, she moved with her son to Chicago in the midst of the Great Depression. Johnson recalled, "We were poor and we didn't like it. We had to go on welfare for about a year and we didn't like that either. Both my mother and I were determined that we weren't going to stay on welfare; we were determined to move out of that category. We worked always toward doing better, toward having a better life. We never had any doubts that we would."[2]

At DuSable High School, named after Jean Baptiste Point du Sable, a black fur trader who founded Chicago when he constructed a trading post there in 1784, Johnson showed his determination to succeed. While working part time for the National Youth Administration, one of the many New Deal programs established during the depression to put people to work, he served as president of the student council, president of his class, editor of the school newspaper, and editor of the class yearbook. He graduated with honors in 1936.

The National Urban League, which had been founded in 1910 to help southern black migrants adjust to life in the northern cities, sponsored a dinner to honor Johnson and other students who had distinguished themselves. The main speaker was Harry H. Pace, president of Supreme Life Insurance Company of America. Johnson approached Pace and told him he had enjoyed the speech. Pace asked about Johnson's plans for the future, and Johnson explained that he would like to go to college but could not afford to do so. Pace offered him a part-time job at Supreme so he could go to college part time.

That September, Johnson enrolled at the University of Chicago and began work at Supreme as an assistant on the *Supreme Liberty Guardian*, the company's magazine. Applying his high school editorial experience, he quickly took on more and more responsibility. When he was named editor of the *Guardian*, he quit college to devote himself to the magazine full time.

Johnson knew what he wanted to do. He formed his own Johnson

Publishing Company and began to publish *Negro Digest*. Circulation grew slowly until he had the idea of a series entitled, "If I Were A Negro," in which prominent whites imagined being black. First Lady Eleanor Roosevelt was among those who contributed articles to the series, which caused circulation to jump markedly.

In November 1945, Johnson launched a second magazine, *Ebony*, a monthly aimed at showing that blacks led successful, middle-class lives. He eventually succeeded in attracting white advertisers by showing that black Americans were consumers, too.

In 1950, Johnson discontinued *Negro Digest* (he would revive it ten years later as *Black World*) and started *Tan*, an advice magazine. *Tan* was incorporated in 1971 into a magazine featuring black entertainers. The following year, he began to publish *Jet*, a pocket-size weekly newsmagazine.

In 1972, Johnson became the first black publisher to receive the magazine industry's most prestigious honor, the Magazine Publishers Association's Henry Johnson Fisher Award, for outstanding contributions to publishing. In accepting the award, he said, "We have to

THE START-UP

Among Johnson's duties as editor of the *Guardian* was to read as many magazines and newspapers as possible and to make a digest of articles about black people. This gave him the idea of publishing a magazine for general black audiences.

When he could not interest anyone in backing the idea, he decided to go directly to the public for start-up money. Using his mother's furniture as security for a $500 loan, he mailed 20,000 copies of a letter offering charter subscriptions to his new magazine. Three thousand people sent in the $2 annual subscription fee, giving Johnson $6,000 to start his venture.

Preparing to run Johnson Enterprises, Linda Johnson Rice, shown here with her father, earned an M.B.A. degree (Master's in Business Administration) from Northwestern University's Kellogg School of Business. (AP/Wide World Photos)

anticipate what the reader will want tomorrow by walking a step ahead of him. In fact, we have to anticipate the reader's desires and wishes by leading him, step by step, to what he really wants."[3]

Practicing what he preached, Johnson branched out into other projects, including a book division and a book club, a travel service, the Ebony Fashion Fair, Supreme Beauty Products Company, and Fashion Fair Cosmetics. In the summer of 1972, Johnson's purchase of radio station WGRT made him the first African American in Chicago to own a broadcasting outlet.

In addition to the ventures he started on his own, Johnson invested in others. He is a major shareholder in Supreme Life Insurance Company, where he got his start, as well as in *Essence*, the magazine for black women. In 1982, the prestigious business magazine *Forbes* named him to its list of the 400 richest Americans.

John H. Johnson married Eunice Walker in 1941. Mrs. Johnson is now secretary-treasurer and director of the Ebony Fashion Fair business. The couple adopted two children, John Harold and Linda. John Harold died at age twenty-five of sickle-cell anemia, the chronic hereditary blood disease that occurs primarily among people of African descent. Linda, who was only seven years old when she first toured the fashion capitals of Europe with her mother, would one day head Johnson Publishing Company.

DEMPSEY J.
TRAVIS

(B. 1920)

✦

Like John H. Johnson, a fellow alumnus of Chicago's DuSable High School, Dempsey J. Travis was always motivated "to do better than ever." He was born February 25, 1920, in Chicago, the son of Louis Travis, an unskilled laborer who worked in the stockyards, and Minnie Travis. At the time, Chicago had many new black residents from the South, lured by the promise of jobs in World War I and a better life in the North. They brought their culture with them, and Chicago became a creative center for the blues and jazz.

Young Dempsey Travis started playing the piano when he was four years old. At the age of fifteen, he formed his own band and began playing at local dances. Only a year later, he was accepted into the musicians' union, becoming one of the youngest professional bandleaders in the city. Even after being drafted into the army in 1942, he continued his musical career. At Camp Custer, Michigan, he formed a small combo and played off-post gigs, musicians' slang for jobs.

In 1948, after World War II had ended, President Harry S. Truman

barred discrimination in the armed forces, giving blacks more opportunities to serve as officers and in combat roles. Travis completed Quartermaster School for Non-Commissioned Officers at Camp Lee, Virginia, and was sent to Maryland to work as a clerk at the Camp Aberdeen Proving Ground Post Exchange, the camp store. Applying the managerial skills he had used as a bandleader, in less than a year Travis was made supervisor of all army stores in the area.

Honorably discharged from the army, Travis returned to Chicago to enroll at Roosevelt University. But he was not expecting what happened next. He flunked the entrance exam. He suddenly realized that although he had graduated from high school with good grades, his education was not good enough.

Travis tried without success to revive his old combo. He even worked briefly in the stockyards, as his father had before him. Finally, he swallowed his pride and enrolled in night courses in accounting and social science at Englewood High School. He then applied and was accepted at Wilson Junior College, on condition that he take a course in remedial reading. Completing the two-year junior college course in one year, he reapplied to Roosevelt College, and completed the requirements for his bachelor's degree in just one more year. Around that time, he met and married Moselynne Hardwick of Cleveland.

Now that he had his education, what was he going to do? At first, he thought of being a lawyer, but Dempsey Travis really wanted to go into business for himself, so he started Travis Realty Company in 1949. It was rough at first, but, like many great entrepreneurs, he eventually managed to make it work by recognizing what people need. As a real estate broker, Travis realized that white-owned banks and mortgage firms were reluctant to give mortgages to blacks to enable them to buy homes. In order to

◆ A **mortgage** is a pledge to repay a loan, usually on expensive property such as a house.

address that need, he founded the Sivart (Travis spelled backward) Mortgage Corporation.

Travis's timing was perfect. In 1960, President John F. Kennedy appointed Dr. Robert C. Weaver to head the Department of Housing and Urban Development. Weaver, the first African American to hold that post, immediately began to remove obstacles for blacks in housing. Sivart Mortgage Corporation benefited from the new climate. Of the more than 2,000 mortgage banking companies in the United States, only twelve were owned by blacks. By the early 1970s, Sivart had become the largest and most influential of the black-owned companies.

Travis branched out, forming Freeway Mortgage and Investment Company and Dempsey J. Travis Securities and Investment Company. He and others founded Seaway National Bank in Chicago. Seaway's business expanded rapidly, and by the early 1990s, it had become the largest black-owned bank in the United States.

In addition to running his multifaceted businesses, Travis published several books. But he did not take his success for granted. As a reminder, he hung his Roosevelt diploma on the wall behind his desk, next to the framed letter of rejection from Roosevelt's dean of admissions.

BERRY
GORDY JR.

(B. 1929)

✦

Famous as the Motor City, automobile capital of the world, Detroit, Michigan, also became famous for black musical talent, thanks in large measure to the entrepreneur Berry Gordy Jr.

Born on November 28, 1929, on Detroit's lower East Side, Gordy was one of Berry Sr. and Bertha I. Gordy's eight children. Growing up, Berry Jr.'s two greatest loves were boxing and jazz. By the time he graduated from Northeastern High School in 1948, he was ready to put boxing first and follow in the footsteps of other blacks who had made a success in the boxing world, such as Joe Louis. Fighting as a featherweight, he actually had fifteen Golden Gloves matches before he was drafted into the United States Army.

Honorably discharged in 1953 after serving in the conflict in Korea, Gordy married Thelma Coleman. They had three children, Hazel Joy, Berry, and Terry. Gordy was too old to continue his boxing career, so he switched to his other love and opened a record store that specialized in jazz. Unfortunately, he had failed to notice that blacks in Detroit were not especially interested in jazz. They were much more

interested in rock and roll. Berry Gordy's 3-D Record Mart went bankrupt after only two years.

Gordy reluctantly went to work in Detroit's major industry, nailing upholstery in Lincoln automobiles. But his heart was still in music. After his record store closed, he began to listen to rock and roll to see what all the fuss was about. He and his sister Gwen wrote several songs in the new style, which they tried to sell to local singers and music labels.

The singer Jackie Wilson liked their work, and his recording of their song "Reet Petite" was their first success. Gordy and Gwen also wrote four other songs that became early hits for Wilson: "Lonely Teardrops," released by Brunswick Records in 1958, was the most famous. Based on that success, Gordy quit his $85-a-week job in the automobile plant and struck out on his own as an independent producer.

But even as a writer of hit songs, Berry Gordy Jr. was in no way financially secure. He later explained, "As a writer, I had problems getting money at the time that I needed it. I was broke even with hit records in certain cases. When the companies paid me, it was three months later and I owed out to the family."[1]

Once, a New York publisher did not pay him, and a lawyer advised him not to bother to sue the company. The case would be tied up for months, and the legal fees alone would be more than what the publisher owed him. Gordy learned an important lesson about business: If you have no control, you have no power.

When Gordy's sister Anna formed her own record label, Anna Records, he saw a way to gain the control he needed. Borrowing $800 from his family, Gordy founded his own record company, Hitsville, USA, an umbrella, or controlling, company under which he established a second company, Jobete Music Company, Inc., and various labels, such as Tamla. He and Anna decided to work together.

In 1970, Berry Gordy left Detroit and moved his company's headquarters to Hollywood, California, the heart of the entertainment industry. He established a motion picture division whose first film, *Lady Sings the Blues*, a biography of the singer Billie Holiday, starred Diana Ross. He also made plans to produce Broadway shows, television specials, and television movies. In 1973, Gordy resigned as

IS THERE A FORMULA FOR SUCCESS?

Yes, there are many formulas for success. Gordy was familiar with the workings of Chess, an independent, family-run record company in Chicago, and he copied what seemed to him to be Chess's winning formula—to find and groom local talent and write contracts with that talent that benefited the company.

There was a great deal of talent in Detroit's black community. The first artist Gordy signed was a teenager named William "Smokey" Robinson, who had a group called the Miracles. Soon, other young black kids were coming to Gordy. For every new act he accepted, he turned dozens away. He signed up groups such as the Marvelettes and the Contours and the Primes, whose name he changed to the Temptations. And he signed up individuals such as Mary Wells and a nine-year-old blind boy named Stevie Morris, who later became known as Stevie Wonder. In 1962, Gordy produced no fewer than five hit records and changed the name of his company to Motown, a contraction of the words Motor Town.

That same year he finally agreed to give a contract to the Supremes, a female group that had started singing as the Primettes, a sister group for the Primes (who became the Temptations). As with his other homegrown performers, Gordy groomed the three young women carefully, insisting that they take courses in etiquette, makeup, clothing, and choreography. With Diana Ross in the lead, the Supremes' tenth single, "Where Did Our Love Go?" hit the top of the charts, and they went on to become one of the most successful acts in history.

✦ A **contract** is a written agreement between individuals or groups.

Many Motown stars were brought to the company by other stars. Diana Ross discovered the Jackson Five, whose youngest member was Michael Jackson.

Berry Gordy's Motown sound, headlined in 1967 by the hit-making Supremes (clockwise from left, Diana Ross, Mary Wilson, and Cindy Birdsong), captured a huge interracial audience. (National Archives)

president of Motown Records to head Motown Industries, a huge umbrella corporation overseeing all of his enterprises.

In 1988, Gordy was inducted into the Rock and Roll Hall of Fame. That same year, he sold Motown Records to MCA, retaining the rights to the classic Motown songs. In 1997, he sold a half-stake in the publishing company that owns the rights to classic Motown songs to EMI Music Publishing. He hoped to spend more time writing songs and working with the newly established Motown Historical Museum in Detroit. "I've not been happy doing all the business stuff," he explained. "Now I can get back to the fun."[2]

QUINCY
JONES

(B. 1933)

✦

Quincy Delight Jones was only thirteen when he picked up a trumpet and joined a small Seattle, Washington, musical group formed by the blind singer-pianist Ray Charles, who was also a teenager. When the great jazz singer Billie Holiday arrived in Seattle to perform, the young Jones played trumpet in her backup band. According to Jones, "Seattle was the last stopping ground before people took off for the Pacific. It was the hottest, jumpingest place in America."[1]

How did Jones arrive in Seattle? The story began on a sad note. Born on March 14, 1933, in Chicago, Illinois, Quincy Jones was only three years old when he and his older brother, Lloyd, watched as their mother was carried away to a state mental institution. Their father, who later remarried, moved the entire family to Seattle when Quincy was ten. Quincy's life began to improve.

A composer by age fifteen, Jones learned that bandleader Lionel Hampton was playing a gig in Seattle, and he went backstage at the theater to show Hampton his suite *The Four Winds*. Hampton was so

impressed by the young Jones's talent that he hired him to play third trumpet in his band while they were in Seattle.

On graduation from high school, Jones earned a scholarship to study with jazz trumpeter Clark Terry in Boston at a conservatory later known as the Berklee School of Music. Jones took ten subjects per day and at night played gigs to pay his room rent. After two years, ready to start a career as a full-time musician, he went to New York. Because he and Lionel Hampton had kept in touch, Jones got an offer in 1953 to accompany Hampton's band to Europe as both a trumpet player and an arranger.

After the Hampton band's European tour was over, Jones remained in Paris to study with Nadia Boulanger, the French musicologist whose former students included the great American composers Leonard Bernstein and Aaron Copland. Returning to the United States, Jones worked as an arranger for the jazz singer Dinah Washington before being hired as musical director for a blues opera. When the show folded, Jones decided to take the all-star jazz orchestra he had assembled for the show on tour to Europe.

That was a big mistake. They had no advance plan and were unable to find work. The orchestra was stranded for ten months, and the twenty-four-year-old Quincy Jones seriously contemplated suicide. He had learned a valuable lesson the hard way, but he stayed on his feet, and his luck eventually changed.

Mercury Records offered Jones a job, and within three years, he had been promoted to vice president, making him one of the first black executives at a major white-owned record company.

But Jones had more in his vision of the future than a salaried job. While working for Mercury, he continued composing and playing. He was among the first blacks to break into the business of writing scores for motion pictures. By the middle 1990s, he had composed more than thirty film scores, including those for *In the Heat of the Night* and *Roots*.

THE PARTNER

Jones's business partner, the Warner company, merged with another giant company, Time, Inc., to form the massive conglomerate Time Warner, Inc., in 1989. Jones did not miss a beat. He formed Quincy Jones Entertainment Company in partnership with a division of Time Warner, Inc., to produce television shows and movies. Among the television shows produced by Quincy Jones Entertainment Company were *In the House* and *Fresh Prince of Bel Air*, which ran for six seasons. The company also co-produced with Steven Spielberg the 1985 film adaptation of Alice Walker's novel *The Color Purple*.

> ✦ A **conglomerate** is a group of widely varied companies joined under one ownership.
>
> ✦ **Leverage**, like the action of a lever, is whatever means you use to give you added strength to achieve a goal.

Jones believes that the key to success in business is to have partnerships with major companies. "Power…is about leverage," he says. "If you can demand things on your own terms, then you are winning the game; otherwise, you are playing by other people's rules."[2]

In 1974, Jones had surgery to remove two life-threatening brain aneurysms. His horn-playing days were over, but his brush with death only spurred him to accomplish more. He had always wanted to work for himself. In 1980, he discovered how he could do it in a big way—he formed his own record label, Qwest Records, in equal partnership with Warner Records. His experience, talent, and insistence on control, backed up by his powerful partnership with Warner, would be unbeatable.

From the first, Jones decided to follow his own broad musical interests. Other black-owned labels recorded exclusively for one audience and in one style. Jones's artists' styles ran from rock and roll to rhythm and blues to jazz to gospel. He had the ability to move in and out of different circles, to work with many different types of people, and to identify new styles.

By the time Quincy Jones celebrated his fiftieth year in the music business in 1996, he had racked up so many Emmy and Grammy awards that he could no longer keep track of them. He also owned five separate enterprises. In addition to those already mentioned, he is a partner in one of the largest minority-owned broadcasting companies, Qwest Broadcasting, a collaboration with the Tribune Company, which has television stations in Atlanta and New Orleans. In 1993, fed up with rock music magazines that virtually ignored rap music, Jones launched his own magazine, *Vibe*. His next frontier is electronic publishing.

Married and divorced three times (his wives have been Jeri Caldwell, his high school sweetheart; Ula Anderson, a Swedish model; and Peggy Lipton, an actress), Jones has several children and grandchildren.

EARL G.
GRAVES

(B. 1935)

✦

Earl G. Graves recalls that his father "used to say he wanted me to *own* something."[1] The elder Graves died when Earl was nineteen, but Earl grew up to make his father's dream a reality.

Graves was born January 9, 1935, in the Bedford-Stuyvesant section of Brooklyn, New York, to Earl Godwin Graves and Winifred Sealy Graves. His father worked as a shipping clerk. Young Earl Graves showed early entrepreneurial interests, selling $150 worth of Christmas cards when he was only five. He graduated from the predominantly white Erasmus Hall High School, as his father had before him, and then enrolled at Morgan State College in Baltimore, Maryland.

Graves's father died while he was at Morgan State, and he had to get a job to put himself through school. He worked summers as a lifeguard in Brooklyn. During the school year, he operated several businesses on campus, including a food service and a flower, gardening, and landscaping enterprise. At Morgan State, Graves joined the Reserve Officers Training Corps, and immediately after receiving his

B.A. in economics in 1958, he entered the U.S. Army, where he rose to the rank of captain in the 19th Special Forces Group, the famous Green Berets. While in the army, Graves married Barbara Kydd, who later worked beside him to build his businesses.

After leaving the army, Graves returned to Bedford-Stuyvesant and worked in a real estate company, becoming manager of the company within a year. In 1965, he offered his services as a volunteer with the staff of New York State Senator Robert F. Kennedy, and a year later joined the staff full time with the responsibility of planning and supervising events. He was still an assistant to Kennedy in 1968, when the senator was assassinated.

In 1968, Graves started his own business, Earl G. Graves Associates, a management consulting firm specializing in assistance to small businesses. But his dream was to start the first African American business magazine. In 1970, he borrowed $150,000 from the Manhattan Capital Corporation to found Earl G. Graves Publishing Company, Inc., and to start *Black Enterprise* magazine.

BREAKING DOWN THE BARRIERS

Opportunities for black business enterprises were ripe in the 1970s. Presidents Lyndon B. Johnson and Richard M. Nixon attempted to address the problems of racism by supporting the growth of black business. In 1964, under the Johnson administration, the Office of Minority Business Enterprise was created within the Small Business Administration. Five years later, President Nixon, although not a particular friend of civil rights, became the first president to issue an executive order calling for more minority business opportunities.

The legal end of segregation in many areas of life in the 1960s further enabled more blacks to start a wide range of businesses. *Black Enterprise* magazine filled an important need for advice and information and was an immediate success.

Black Enterprise *is an award-winning monthly magazine about African Americans who are succeeding in business today. (Earl G. Graves, Ltd.)*

Some of the features Graves introduced to the magazine became nationally known, such as his annual list of the top 100 black-owned businesses and the *Black Enterprise* Achievement Awards for successful black entrepreneurs. Advertising by multinational corporations greatly increased the profits of the magazine.

Graves used what he learned and the profits from his magazine

WHAT DOES IT TAKE TO BE AN ENTREPRENEUR?

In *How to Succeed in Business without Being White*, Earl Graves offers this list of traits that he believes most entrepreneurs have in common:

1. A "junkyard dog" mentality—they won't let go.
2. A willingness to take a risky leap, but only after a good look.
3. A talent for focusing on solutions rather than problems.
4. A high level of energy.
5. The drive to make money so that they can make more money.
6. A talent for starting companies, but not necessarily for managing them.
7. Flexibility.
8. An abundance of courage.

to establish other companies, including EGG Dallas Broadcasting, Inc.; B.C.I. Marketing, Inc., a development firm; a marketing firm; and a distribution firm. In 1990, Graves entered into a partnership with basketball star Earvin "Magic" Johnson to purchase a $60 million Pepsi-Cola franchise in Washington, D.C.—the largest minority-owned Pepsi franchise in the United States.

One of the most influential black entrepreneurs of his time, Graves was active in TransAfrica, a lobbying group that encouraged investment in democratic African nations and sought to end the legal segregation known as apartheid in South Africa by urging American corporations not to invest in business there. When South Africa ended apartheid, and Nelson Mandela became its president, Graves organized a group of African American business leaders who invested millions of dollars in a new business venture there.

At this point in his career, what does Earl Graves consider to be his greatest achievement? In his book, *How to Succeed in Business without Being White*, he says it is the fact that his sons—Earl Jr. ("Butch"), John, and Michael—all work for the family business and want to build upon what he and their mother started.

REGINALD F.
LEWIS

(1942–1993)

◆

One of Reginald Lewis's earliest childhood memories was of hearing his grandparents talk about discrimination. When he was asked how he felt about it, the six-year-old Reginald replied simply, "Why should white guys have all the fun?"[1] Forty years later, he would preside over a vast commercial empire spanning four continents and have personal wealth estimated by *Forbes* magazine at more than $400 million.

Reginald Francis Lewis was born on December 7, 1942, in East Baltimore, Maryland. Shortly after Reginald's birth, Clinton Lewis, his father, who had operated several small businesses, joined the navy. Reginald was five when his twenty-two-year-old mother, Carolyn Cooper Lewis, divorced his father and took Reginald to live with her parents. They arrived in the middle of night, and Reginald would always remember his grandfather complaining about having two more mouths to feed and his mother insisting that they would not be a burden and would pay their way.

Lewis got his first job, a paper route, when he was ten. From that

time on, he always had at least one job. By the time he was in high school and working in the restaurant of a local country club, he had set his goal in life: Despite having mediocre grades, he planned to be the richest black man in America.

Lewis attended Virginia State College in Petersburg, Virginia, on a football scholarship and majored in business administration. His grades were still poor. When in the spring of 1965 he learned of a special summer school for black students established by Harvard Law School, he was convinced that this was his "shot at the big time." He lobbied energetically and successfully to be among the five students selected by Virginia State to attend. That summer, he made such a strong impression on his professors that not long after he returned to Virginia State for his senior year, he was offered a place in the Harvard Law School class of 1968.

Frightened by the fiercely competitive atmosphere—and perhaps also by the fact that of the more than 500 students in the freshman class, fewer than twenty were black—Lewis's grades suffered during his first year. By the end of his third year, however, he had moved up to B's. He did far more than study at Harvard. He was single-minded in his efforts to "improve himself" by reading classic literature and listening to all kinds of music. In the summer after his freshman year, he took a Harvard charter trip to Europe and fell in love with Paris.

When he graduated, Lewis had job offers from law firms in both Baltimore and New York City. He chose a firm in New York and went to work in its corporate law department. He met his future wife, Loida Nicholas, on a blind date. They were married in her native Philippines in August 1969.

Less than two years after joining the New York law firm, Lewis left to join a fellow Harvard Law School graduate and a handful of other attorneys in starting Wallace, Murphy, Thorpe, and Lewis, one of the first, if not the first, black law firms on Wall Street. From the start, Lewis proved the most adept at attracting new business, and he also

WHAT'S THE HARDEST PART OF BEING AN ENTREPRENEUR?

In Lewis's autobiography, *Why Should White Guys Have All the Fun?*, he wrote: "I had to guard against being too easy or too hard on myself....The hardest fact to come to grips with was that many of your strengths can indeed be weaknesses at different stages in the deal process. For example, in Almet, I was the finder of the deal, chief financial analyst, fund-raiser, quasi-legal officer, and chief strategist. In short, I was going about it...backwards.

For five years, I had gone about it all wrong, using an approach that could get me close, but not get the job done. A hard pill to swallow."

acquired a vast body of knowledge about how to structure corporate acquisitions.

✦ **Corporate acquisition** occurs when one company purchases another with stock, cash, or a combination of both.

Lewis lost out on his first two personal attempts at acquiring companies: In 1975, he tried to buy Parks Sausage (see page 111), and in 1977, he tried to buy Almet, a company that made leisure furniture. His failures were learning experiences.

Lewis was successful in purchasing a radio station in the U.S. Virgin Islands in 1982, and he established what he optimistically called the Caribbean Basin Broadcasting Network. But the station lost money, and he sold it in 1986.

In 1987, Lewis succeeded in buying McCall Pattern Company, a designer, manufacturer, and marketer of patterns for home sewing that had been established in 1870 and was the second-largest company in the business. Because fewer women were sewing at home, the company's sales had been declining for some years, and Lewis felt he could get it at a bargain price.

It took him four years from the time he first read an article about McCall's to get ready to make his move. In 1983, he created TLC Pattern, Inc., and TLC Group, Inc., for the express purpose of taking over McCall's. He then set about obtaining the multimillion-dollar loans he would need for the financing, and he eventually landed a commitment for $19 million from Bankers Trust Company. He obtained most of the rest—$3.5 million—from members of McCall's top management in exchange for shares in the company under his ownership.

Under Lewis, McCall's signed up celebrities Brooke Shields, Diahann Carroll, and Shari Belafonte-Harper to advertise their own designs for the company. Lewis raised the prices and income doubled. In 1987, he sold McCall's for $65 million.

Lewis then turned around and bought Beatrice International, a giant food conglomerate with sixty-four companies in thirty-one countries. To do so, he arranged a $1 billion loan from Drexel Burnham Lambert, a United States investment banking firm. On December 1, 1987, he closed the deal, having pulled off the largest buyout of its kind in history.

Lewis now owned an international business with annual revenues of $2.5 billion, which far surpassed those of John H. Johnson's Johnson Publishing Company. Lewis was the owner of the largest African American–run business in the world.

Lewis enjoyed his far-flung empire. He acquired a private, corporate jet and spent most of his time flying from one international site to another. He purchased a home in Paris and moved his family there, and he made a special point of never missing a parent-teacher association meeting or recital at the international school in which his daughters enrolled. He also spent time studying the most effective ways to share some of his wealth, and in 1987, he created the Reginald F. Lewis Foundation. Within four years, the foundation had awarded $10 million in grants to educational, civil rights, medical, and artistic institutions in the United States.

Beginning in 1990, Lewis complained of tiredness, and he died on January 19, 1993, six weeks after his brain tumor was diagnosed. His widow, Loida, mourned for a year. Then in early 1994, she stepped in to lead the company. Before his death, Reginald Lewis had written a letter to Loida and their daughters in which he had expressed his vision for the company. Loida believed it was her responsibility to make his vision real.

By 1995, Loida Lewis was No. 1 on *Working Woman* magazine's list of the top fifty women business owners. Her older daughter, Leslie, joined the board of directors of Beatrice International.

OPRAH
WINFREY

(B. 1954)

◆

In the 1950s and in every decade thereafter, more and more African American families struggled to stay together through their personal and financial difficulties. The fortunate ones managed to protect their children from their problems. Others could not. Oprah Gail Winfrey's parents were among those who struggled.

Oprah Winfrey was born in Kosciusko, Mississippi, on January 29, 1954. She was supposed to have been named Orpah, after the sister-in-law of Ruth in the Old Testament, but the letters were reversed on her birth certificate, and Oprah she became. Oprah's young, unmarried parents, Vernon Winfrey and Vernita Lee, were unable to take care of her, and she was raised on a farm by her father's mother, Hattie Mae Winfrey.

As a child, Winfrey amused herself by performing for an "audience" of farm animals and corncob dolls. She learned to talk early, could read by the age of three, and was able to recite short speeches in church. Her grandmother was strict but kind, and Winfrey credits

her with giving her the strength and sense of reason that she feels were the secrets of her later success.

After six years, Oprah's mother sent for her, and Oprah went to live with her mother in a housing project in Milwaukee, Wisconsin. But it was a brief, unhappy reunion, and Oprah soon went to Nashville, Tennessee, to be with her father and his wife, Velma. For one short, happy year, Oprah felt secure. She blossomed as she had in Mississippi, doing well at school and giving recitations at church and social functions. But then her mother wanted her back, and her father reluctantly complied.

Winfrey's mother had other children by then, and she worked hard to take care of them. She was too busy, unfortunately, to give Oprah the attention she needed—or to protect her from male friends and relatives. As an adolescent, Oprah Winfrey was abused by several men she trusted, and in her confusion and fear of telling what had happened, she became a serious discipline problem. She lied, stole from her mother, ran away from home, and very nearly wound up in a detention center. To avoid that, her desperate mother sent her back to her father in Nashville.

Vernon Winfrey, a barber by trade, was by this time a city councilman in Nashville. A strict disciplinarian, like his mother, he took his daughter in hand and turned her life around. She earned excellent grades at East Nashville High School, was elected president of the student council, and at sixteen, won an Elks Club oratorical contest that guaranteed her a full college scholarship. In that same year, she was chosen as one of the Outstanding Teenagers of America. The following year, 1971, she entered and won both the Miss Black Nashville and Miss Black Tennessee beauty pageants. Climbing up this stairway of successes, she left her childhood as far behind as she could.

Winfrey was still in high school when she entered broadcasting and began reading the news for WVOL-Radio in Nashville. She discovered the world of television in her sophomore year at Tennessee

State University, a black college where she majored in drama and speech.

After graduating, Winfrey started out on WJZ-TV in Baltimore, Maryland. Its morning show, *Baltimore Is Talking,* revealed Winfrey's real calling—communicating with her audience on so-called soft news, such as family and lifestyle issues. After seven successful years as a Baltimore talk show host, she accepted an offer from WLS-TV in Chicago to host *A.M. Chicago.* She soon owned the airwaves in her time slot.

In 1985, *A.M. Chicago* became *The Oprah Winfrey Show,* and it went into national syndication the following year. It soon outdistanced all similar talk shows, and eleven years later, it was still the highest rated in what by then had become an overcrowded field of imitators.

Winfrey had proven her strength many times over in other ways as well. In 1984, she began her acting career, playing the role of the tough, proud, tragic Sophie in the 1985 film *The Color Purple* and winning both a Golden Globe Award and an Academy Award nomination. In 1985, she formed her own production company, Harpo Productions (Oprah spelled backward), to produce videos and films of social importance and to control her syndicated television program. In so doing, she became the first black woman and only the third woman in the United States to own a television and film production studio. Her annual income from her various entertainment projects is estimated at more than $40 million.

Winfrey has made big financial gifts to Spelman and Morehouse Colleges in Atlanta, Georgia. She stresses education in other ways, such as by taking part in American Library Association programs to encourage reading and by launching a television book club for her viewers. Her memories of childhood have also led her to support efforts to stop child abuse.

S H E L T O N   J A C K S O N   " S P I K E "
LEE

(B. 1957)

✦

Like the pioneer, Oscar Micheaux, Spike Lee made his mark as an entrepreneur by taking the risks necessary to make films based on African American life. By the late twentieth century, life was not nearly as harsh for blacks as it was when Micheaux was growing up. But in some ways, it was just as hard to succeed, although more people had the chance to try and the rewards were often much greater.

Born Shelton Jackson Lee on March 20, 1957, in Atlanta, Georgia, Spike got his nickname from his mother because he was a tough little guy. His mother, Jacquelyn Shelton Lee, was an art and literature teacher. His father, William, was a jazz composer and musician. When Spike was two years old, the family moved to Brooklyn, New York, where the four other Lee children were born: Chris, David, Joy (she later changed the spelling to Joie), and Cinque.

Spike was raised in a very comfortable, artistic atmosphere. Through his father, he learned to appreciate jazz and folk music at an early age and met many great musicians and singers in both styles. All the children had music lessons. His mother took him to art galleries,

museums, and plays and encouraged him to read literature by black writers.

Lee attended integrated New York City public schools. But, on graduation from John Dewey High School in Brooklyn, Lee entered Morehouse College in Atlanta, as his father and grandfather had done (his mother and grandmother had graduated from its sister school, Spelman College). Being in an all-black environment gave him both a sense of power and a sense of unfairness. He discovered that color prejudice was just as strong among blacks as it was among whites.

In 1977, Lee was in his sophomore year at Morehouse when his mother died suddenly from cancer. The following summer, he bought a super-8 video camera and noodled around taking footage of his family and friends. He may unconsciously have wanted to capture them on film—to have something of them that could not be lost, as his mother had been lost to him.

In his junior year, Spike went to see Michael Cimino's film *The Deer Hunter*. By the time the film was over, Spike Lee had decided what he wanted to do with his life: he wanted to make films.

Spike was concerned that there were few blacks in Hollywood working behind the cameras—as producers, directors, cameramen. He dreamed of ushering in a new era of black filmmaking in Hollywood.

Lee received his master's degree in filmmaking from New York University Tisch School of the Arts in 1983, but no job offers awaited him. So, he decided to become an independent filmmaker. He managed to raise $40,000 to begin filming the story of a young black bicycle messenger. He formed his own production company, Forty Acres and a Mule Filmworks, but problems with financing and a dispute with the Screen Actors' Guild forced him to cancel the project.

Undaunted, Lee tried again. He made his next film, *She's Gotta Have It*, with help from the New York State Council on the Arts and a total budget of $175,000 (peanuts, by Hollywood standards), mostly

WHERE DO IDEAS COME FROM?

Lee had this to say about ideas in his book *Do the Right Thing*:

> "It's amazing to me how ideas come. Any time, any place, and whapp!...Lightning strikes and it's there. The 'it' is that initial kernel that is developed, thought over, and dissected, again and again.

> "While I'm putting the finishing touches on one film, I'm thinking about the next Spike Lee joint....Then wham, presto, change-o! It's time to start writing again."

investments by friends. Although he had his hands full directing, acting in, and editing the film, he also exploited its marketing possibilities. He kept a journal of the film, from initial ideas to final production notes, and published it in 1987. *She's Gotta Have It*, released in 1986, was a huge success, winning the Prix de la Jeunesse (Young Director's Prize) at the Cannes Film Festival.

On a virtual shoestring, he made the 1988 *School Daze*, and based on its success, he secured a larger budget for *Do the Right Thing*. This film about racial tensions between blacks and Italians in a Brooklyn neighborhood won rave reviews and generated considerable controversy. It also secured Lee's place as an important new director and blazed the trail in Hollywood for other young black directors to follow.

Lee directed nine films in ten years. The most famous of the later films is the three-hour-plus *Malcolm X* (1992). Lee expanded his other entrepreneurial pursuits as well. A smart businessman, he has invested his profits wisely. He has a range of businesses to attend to, including a record label and a clothing line. He is a millionaire many times over.

Lee also used his money to endow a scholarship for minority students at NYU's Tisch School of the Arts.

Lee met Tanya Lynette Lewis, a practicing attorney in Washington, D.C., in 1992, and they married the following year. They named their first child, a daughter, Satchel, after Leroy "Satchel" Paige, the great pitcher of the Negro baseball leagues.

ALPHONSE "BUDDY"
FLETCHER JR.

(B. 1966)

✦

Alphonse "Buddy" Fletcher, the eldest of three sons, was brought up in Waterford, Connecticut. His father was a technician at General Dynamics but at heart was an entrepreneur. At various times, Fletcher's father operated a chicken restaurant, ran a moving business, and owned a couple of apartment buildings.

Fletcher's mother was an elementary school principal who earned extra money working as a licensed real estate broker. Recalls Fletcher, "They were very motivated, very busy, very entrepreneurial and creative. I think that had a large impact [on me]."[1]

Buddy Fletcher attended public schools and was a serious student. In high school, he was on the football team, but he always made sure to do his homework at night, no matter how tired he was.

Fletcher was also smart and impatient. At the age of eleven, he created a program on his computer that could predict the outcome of dog races with up to 80 percent accuracy, but those odds weren't good enough for him. He wanted 100 percent accuracy. At Harvard University, where he majored in applied mathematics, he and his

roommate started a small T-shirt business. But sales were slower than Fletcher had anticipated, so as soon as he had earned back his initial investment, he sold his share of the business to his partner.

Fletcher enrolled in Air Force R.O.T.C. (Reserve Officers Training Corps) while at Harvard and intended to serve at least four years as an officer in the military. As a child, he had loved playing with G.I. Joe toys. But Air Force budget cuts reduced the number of new recruits, so Fletcher needed a new idea for a career. A college friend suggested that he use his mathematical skills to become a stock trader on Wall Street, and when he graduated in 1987, Fletcher got a job as a trading associate with the brokerage firm Bear, Stearns. There he worked with a group that used math and computers to figure out trading moves. He made enough of a mark to be offered a job at another brokerage firm, Kidder, Peabody.

According to Fletcher, the firm of Kidder, Peabody offered him a substantial salary plus a percentage of the profits he made. At the end of the year, Fletcher received 10 percent of the profits he had made for the company, but that was much smaller than the amount he expected. He resigned, and sued the company for going back on its promise. In 1992, a New York panel awarded Fletcher $1,260,000 in back pay from Kidder, Peabody.

Fletcher had won, but he now had a reputation on Wall Street as a troublemaker. Aware that he might have difficulty finding another job, he decided to go into business on his own. He rented temporary office space at his old firm, Bear, Stearns, bought a computer, and prepared a proposal for a $100 million trade. Within a few days, he found a buyer and completed the trade on that buyer's behalf. This time he could keep all the profit.

He moved into his own offices and established Fletcher Asset Management. By 1996, he had twenty-five employees. The firm had established a reputation for consistency, which is very important in the volatile atmosphere of the stock market.

Fletcher's personal wealth has been estimated at around $50 million. He lives in a luxurious apartment in Manhattan, is driven to work each morning in a chauffeured Mercedes Benz, and he has a personal chef. But he also gives away a lot of his money. In 1993, he pledged $1 million to the National Association for the Advancement of Colored People. The following year, he donated his company's broker-dealer division, Fletcher Capital Markets, to Harvard, a gift worth $4 million.

OMAR
WASOW
(B. 1970)

✦

African Americans such as Omar Wasow are on the cutting edge of new technologies and forms of communication. Still in his twenties, Wasow is a pioneer in cyberspace.

Omar was born on December 22, 1970, in Nairobi, Kenya, where his parents were teaching. Of African American and Jewish descent, from an early age his family and his travels caused him to take a much wider view of the world than most people. Wasow's parents later relocated to New York City, settling in Brooklyn with their son and his sister, Althea. Omar gained admission to Stuyvesant High School in lower Manhattan, for which students must qualify by taking special tests.

Wasow was an early computer user and had a Commodore Vic-20. But at first he did not see the possibilities of the quickly developing new technology for anything besides games and schoolwork. Then one night in Manhattan's Greenwich Village, he attended a party where a widely diverse group of computer buffs gathered. He was fascinated as they swapped stories and software, and he began to see

that technology was a way for people to connect who might never otherwise come in contact with each other.

Wasow went on to Stanford University in California, where he followed his interest in people and designed his own major in race and ethnic relations. One of his favorite people at Stanford was Peta Hoyes, a Jamaican woman who grew up in Queens, New York, and who was one of the few minority mechanical engineering majors there. They shared an interest in technology.

After Stanford, Wasow decided to explore life a little more. He worked on the team of Freedom Summer '92, a 22-city, cross-country voter registration drive. And he also did some international traveling. He was particularly struck by the country of Turkey, with its dramatic architecture, geology, and history. He also became acutely aware that people of African descent were to be found everywhere in the world, and he quickly became fascinated with the concept of the African diaspora, or dispersion, throughout the world.

In the meantime, global communication through computers had developed by leaps and bounds. Nowhere were its creative possibilities being exploited more than in New York City, where Wasow had grown up. So in 1993, Omar Wasow returned home, bringing with him the seeds of an idea to establish a kind of cyberspace Greenwich Village.

For help, he turned to his Stanford friend, Peta Hoyes. The two shared the vision that cyberspace, which was heavily dominated by white males, could be a welcoming place for women and people of color as well. Together, they created New York Online.

As Wasow explained, "We set out to create a service that emphasized smart, thoughtful, and intimate conversation among a diverse group of people. We think New York Online is a bit like the subway in that it's a network that connects you to the whole city and that you are always surrounded by a really eclectic mix of folks."[1]

Wasow's first step was to establish a corporation, Diaspora, Inc., which he incorporated in September 1993. By January 1994, he had set up New York Online (NYO), financing it himself. In NYO's first month of operation, it landed its first consulting client and content developer, Quincy Jones's *Vibe* magazine (see page 134).

From the first, NYO attracted the subscribers Wasow and Hayes were looking for. Roughly 50 percent were minority and 40 percent were female—astounding statistics in white-male-dominated cyberspace.

NYO's growth led to three more businesses—a consumer online service, a web development division, and a new media consulting division.

Still only in his mid-twenties, Wasow by 1996 had become a leading expert in online ventures and was hailed as one of the most influential people to watch in cyberspace. *Newsweek* magazine named him one of its "50 for the Future."

In 1997, Wasow was hired as a commentator by MSNBC, the new television network founded by Microsoft and NBC. One day a week, he joined two other young, hip commentators at a Secaucus, New Jersey, studio for short discussion segments throughout the day that provided context to the news. With his long dreadlocks, he was a certified outsider. But he also wore a suit, because he wanted to be taken seriously. As a young and rising entrepreneur whose web site–building business now counted *Consumer Reports*, *The New Yorker* magazine, and the government of Martinique among its clients and had grossed $400,000 in 1996, he was indeed taken seriously. He planned to write a book, entitled *Cusp*, that would set forth his ideas for his rising generation.

CHRONOLOGY

1742	Marie-Thérèse Metoyer (Coincoin) born
1759	Paul Cuffe born
1762	France cedes all its territory west of the Mississippi River to Spain
1766	James Forten born
	Pierre Toussaint born
1775	First abolition society formed in Philadelphia
1776	Revolutionary War begins
1777	Frank McWorter born
1783	Revolutionary War ends
1784	Black fur trader Jean Baptiste Point du Sable founds a trading post that will become the city of Chicago
1790	First U.S. Patent Act enacted
1791	Thomas L. Jennings born
1800	Sometime after this year, James Forten invents a device to control sails on ships
1803	Haiti becomes an independent black republic
1810	Captain Paul Cuffe sets sail for Sierra Leone with nine black crewmen
	(March 23) First black self-help organization, the New York African Society for Mutual Relief, chartered in New York City
	David Ruggles born
	William A. Leidesdorff born
1812	The War of 1812
1815	Captain Paul Cuffe makes a second trip to Sierra Leone
1816	Marie-Thérèse Metoyer (Coincoin) dies
1817	Colored People's Convention held in Philadelphia
	Paul Cuffe dies
1818	Elizabeth Keckley born

1821	African American freedmen settle Liberia
	(March 3) Thomas L. Jennings patents the "dry scouring" dry cleaning process; believed to be the first African American to receive a patent from an invention
	Mexico wins its independence from Spain
1827	Slavery abolished in New York
1831	Annual Convention of the People of Color held by the National Colored Convention Movement in Philadelphia
1834	David Ruggles opens a bookshop in New York City; considered the nation's first black bookseller
1842	James Forten dies, leaving a sail loft enterprise estimated to be worth $100,000
1843	Richard Henry Boyd born
1845	William A. Leidesdorff appointed U.S. vice-consul to Mexico, probably the first U.S. black diplomat
1848	William A. Leidesdorff dies
1849	David Ruggles dies
1850	Of the nearly 400,000 free blacks in the United States, 3,000 own land
	California becomes the thirty-first U.S. state
1853	Pierre Toussaint dies
1854	Frank McWorter dies
1855	Elizabeth Jennings, sister of Thomas L. Jennings, wins her discrimination suit against New York's Third Avenue Railway Company
1856	Granville T. Woods born
1857	In *Dred Scott* v. *Sanford*, the United States Supreme Court rules against citizenship for blacks
1859	Thomas L. Jennings dies
1861	Civil War begins
1863	Emancipation Proclamation issued by President Abraham Lincoln frees all slaves in the Confederate states
1865	Civil War ends
	President Abraham Lincoln assassinated

1867   Congress passes the first Reconstruction Act, requiring former Confederate states to ratify the "Civil War Amendments," write new constitutions, and grant voting rights to all males, regardless of "race, color, or previous condition of servitude"

Congress passes the Thirteenth Amendment, abolishing slavery in the United States; it is later ratified

Maggie Lena Walker born

Madame C. J. Walker born Sarah McWilliams

1868   Congress passes the Fourteenth Amendment, granting blacks full citizenship and equal rights; it is later ratified

1870   Congress passes the Fifteenth Amendment, granting voting rights to all males

1874   Charles Clinton Spaulding born

1876   Philip A. Payton Jr. born

1877   Reconstruction ends

1884   Granville T. Woods secures his first patent, for an improved steam boiler furnace

Oscar Micheaux born

1892   A. G. Gaston born

1894   Ada "Bricktop" Smith born

1896   In the case *Plessy* v. *Ferguson*, the United States Supreme Court rules that "separate but equal" facilities for blacks are constitutional

1900   Scores of blacks own small businesses; Booker T. Washington forms the National Black Business League

1901   Jake Simmons Jr. born

1902   Granville T. Woods patents an automatic air brake

1903   Maggie Lena Walker becomes the first black woman bank president in America when the St. Luke Penny Savings Bank opens in Richmond, Virginia

1904   Philip A. Payton Jr. founds the Afro-American Realty Co. in Harlem

1907   Elizabeth Keckley dies

Janet Harmon Bragg born

1908   Madame C. J. Walker founds Lelia College in Pittsburgh, Pennsylvania, to teach the Walker System of hair care

1909   National Association for the Advancement of Colored People founded

1910   Granville T. Woods dies

National Urban League founded

1913   Oscar Micheaux publishes his first novel, *The Conquest: The Story of a Negro Pioneer*

1916   Henry G. Parks born

1917   United States enters World War I

Philip A. Payton Jr. dies

1918   John H. Johnson born

1919   Madame C. J. Walker dies

Oscar Micheaux produces his first two films: *The Homesteader* and *Within Our Gates*

1920   Dempsey J. Travis born

1922   Richard Henry Boyd dies

1929   The National Black Business League estimates there are 65,000 black businesses

The stock market crash ushers in the Great Depression

Berry Gordy Jr. born

1930   National Council of Negro Women formed by Maggie Lena Walker and others

1933   Quincy Jones born

1934   Maggie Lena Walker dies

Janet Harmon Bragg earns her private pilot's license

1935   Earl G. Graves born

1941   United States enters World War II

1942   Janet Harmon Bragg awarded her commercial pilot's license

Reginald F. Lewis born

1945   John H. Johnson begins publishing *Ebony* magazine

1949   Dempsey J. Travis founds Travis Realty Company

1951 Oscar Micheaux dies

Henry G. Parks and others found Parks Sausage Company

1952 Charles Clinton Spaulding dies

1954 In the case *Brown* v. *Board of Education of Topeka*, the United States Supreme Court rules that "separate but equal" schools are unconstitutional and orders integration "with all deliberate speed"

Oprah Winfrey born

1957 Shelton Jackson "Spike" Lee born

1958 "Lonely Teardrops," written by Berry Gordy Jr. and his sister Gwen, recorded by Jackie Wilson and released by Brunswick Records

1959 Berry Gordy Jr. founds Motown Records in Detroit, Michigan

1960 Dr. Robert C. Weaver appointed the first African American head of the Department of Housing and Urban Development by President John F. Kennedy

1960s The federal government introduces programs to support black business

1964 The Office of Minority Business Enterprise created within the Small Business Administration under President Lyndon B. Johnson

1966 Alphonse "Buddy" Fletcher born

1968 The Reverend Martin Luther King Jr. assassinated in A. G. Gaston's Lorraine Motel in Memphis, Tennessee

Earl G. Graves forms Earl G. Graves Associates, a management consulting firm

1969 Parks Sausage Company is the first black-owned business to offer its stock to the public

1970 Earl G. Graves founds *Black Enterprise* magazine

Berry Gordy Jr. moves Motown to Hollywood

Omar Wasow born

1970s Dempsey J. Travis's Sivart Mortgage Corporation is the largest and most influential black mortage banking company in the United States

1972 John H. Johnson is the first black publisher to receive the Magazine Publishers Association's Henry Johnson Fisher Award for outstanding contributions to publishing

1980   Quincy Jones forms Qwest Records

1981   Jake Simmons Jr. dies

1982   *Forbes* magazine names John H. Johnson to its list of the 400 richest Americans

1984   Ada "Bricktop" Smith dies

Reginald F. Lewis buys McCall Pattern Company, second largest in the home sewing pattern business, for $22.5 million

1985   *The Oprah Winfrey Show* goes into national syndication

1986   Spike Lee's film *She's Gotta Have It* released

1987   Reginald F. Lewis buys Beatrice International for $985 billion, the largest buyout of its kind in history

1988   Berry Gordy Jr. sells Motown Records to MCA; inducted into the Rock and Roll Hall of Fame

1989   Henry G. Parks dies

Quincy Jones forms Quincy Jones Entertainment Company

1990   Earl G. Graves and Earvin "Magic" Johnson purchase a Pepsi-Cola franchise in Washington, D.C., the largest minority-owned Pepsi franchise in the United States

1992   Alphonse "Buddy" Fletcher establishes Fletcher Asset Management

1990s   Dempsey J. Travis's Seaway National Bank in Chicago becomes the largest black-owned bank in the United States

1993   Janet Harmon Bragg dies

Reginald F. Lewis dies

Quincy Jones launches *Vibe* magazine

1994   Omar Wasow establishes New York Online, a World Wide Web site and web site builder

1996   Oprah Winfrey tops the *Forbes* magazine list of richest celebrities, with $171 million in 1995–1996 earnings

Omar Wasow named by *Newsweek* magazine one of its "50 for the Future"

A. G. Gaston dies

1997   Berry Gordy Jr. sells one-half the Motown classic song catalogue to EMI for $132 million

Omar Wasow joins the new MSNBC television network as a weekly commentator

NOTES

INTRODUCTION

1. Russell L. Adams. *Great Negroes Past and Present*, Third Edition (Chicago: Afro-Am Publishing Co., 1984), 76.

PAUL CUFFE

1. Sidney Kaplan. *The Black Presence in the Era of the American Revolution, 1770–1800* (New York: New York Graphic Society, 1973), 134.

2. Kaplan, *The Black Presence in the Era of the American Revolution*, 133.

3. Kaplan, *The Black Presence in the Era of the American Revolution*, 138–140.

JAMES FORTEN

1. Harry S. Ploski and James Williams, eds. *The Negro Almanac: A Reference Work on the Afro American* (New York: John Wiley & Sons, 1983), 804.

2. Mabel M. Smythe, ed. *The Black American Reference Book* (Englewood Cliffs, NJ: Prentice-Hall, 1976), 543.

3. Dorothy Sterling, ed. *Speak Out in Thunder Tones: Letters and Other Writing by Black Northerners, 1787–1865* (Garden City, NY: Doubleday, 1973), 59.

PIERRE TOUSSAINT

1. "The Quiet Man," *The Anthonian* (June 27, 1976), 4–31.

"FREE FRANK" MCWORTER

1. King James Version of the Bible. Revelation 3:7–8.

THOMAS L. JENNINGS

1. Edgar J. McManus. *A History of Negro Slavery in New York* (Syracuse, NY: Syracuse University Press, 1966), 188.

2. Roi Ottley and William J. Weatherby, eds. *The Negro in New York* (New York: New York Public Library, 1967), 91.

3. Dorothy Sterling, ed. *Speak Out in Thunder Tones: Letters and Other Writings by Black Northerners, 1787–1865* (New York: Doubleday, 1973), 58.

4. John H. Hewitt. "The Search for Elizabeth Jennings, Heroine of a Sunday Afternoon in New York City." *New York History* (Cooperstown, NY: New York State Historical Association, October 1990), 387–415.

DAVID RUGGLES

1. Roi Ottley and William J. Weatherby, eds. *The Negro in New York* (New York: New York Public Library, 1967), 85–86.

2. Ottley and Weatherby, *The Negro in New York*, 87.

3. Ottley and Weatherby, *The Negro in New York*, 86.

ELIZABETH KECKLEY

1. Dorothy Sterling. *We Are Your Sisters: Black Women in the Nineteenth Century* (New York: W. W. Norton, 1984), 251.

GRANVILLE T. WOODS

1. Portia P. James. *The Real McCoy: African-American Invention and Innovation, 1619–1930* (Washington, DC: Smithsonian Institution Press, 1989), 95.

PHILIP A. PAYTON JR.

1. Jervis Anderson. *This Was Harlem, 1900–1950* (New York: Farrar, Straus & Giroux, 1982), 52.

2. Anderson, *This Was Harlem*, 52–53.

A. G. GASTON

1. David Stout. "A. G. Gaston, 103, a Champion of Black Economic Advances," *New York Times* obituary (January 20, 1996), 13.

JANET HARMON BRAGG

1. Janet Harmon Bragg, as told to Marjorie M. Kriz. *Soaring above Setbacks: The Autobiography of Janet Harmon Bragg, African American Aviator* (Washington, DC: Smithsonian Institution Press, 1996), 2.

2. Bragg, *Soaring above Setbacks*, 51.

JOHN H. JOHNSON

1. John H. Johnson, with Lerone Bennett Jr. *Succeeding against the Odds* (New York: Warner Books, 1989), 40.

2. Editors of *Ebony*. *The Ebony Success Library* (3 vols). Volume II: *Famous Blacks Give Secrets of Success* (Nashville, TN: The Southwestern Company, 1973), 133.

3. *The Ebony Success Library*, Volume II, 137.

BERRY GORDY JR.

1. *The Ebony Success Library*, Volume II, 89.

2. Sorkin, Andrew Ross. "Berry Gordy Sells a Stake in Catalogue of Motown Songs," *The New York Times* (July 2, 1997).

QUINCY JONES

1. Michael Kaplan. "On the Record," *American Way* (October 15, 1995), 94.

2. Carolyn M. Brown. "The Master of Trades," *Black Enterprise* (June 1996), 246.

EARL G. GRAVES

1. John N. Ingham. *African-American Business Leaders* (New York: Greenwood Press, 1994), 207.

2. Earl G. Graves. *How to Succeed in Business without Being White*. (New York: HarperCollins, 1997).

REGINALD F. LEWIS

1. Reginald F. Lewis and Blair S. Walker. *"Why Should White Guys Have All the Fun?": How Reginald Lewis Created a Billion-Dollar Business Empire*. (New York: John Wiley & Sons, Inc., 1995), xvii.

ALPHONSE "BUDDY" FLETCHER

1. "The Buddy System," *The New Yorker* (April 29 and May 6, 1996), 83.

OMAR WASOW

1. Noah Green. "The Sixth Borough: A Bulletin Board Grows in Brooklyn," *The Village Voice* (July 12, 1994), 1.

BIBLIOGRAPHY

BOOKS

Adams, Russell L. *Great Negroes Past and Present*. Chicago: Afro-Am Publishing Co. 1984.

Anderson, Jervis. *This Was Harlem, 1900–1950*. New York: Farrar, Straus & Giroux, 1982.

Biography Today, Vol. 1, No. 1 (January 1992); Vol 1, No. 2 (April 1992). Detroit: Omnigraphics, 1992.

Bragg, Janet Harmon, as told to Marjorie M. Kriz. *Soaring above Setbacks: The Autobiography of Janet Harmon Bragg, African American Aviator*. Washington, D.C.: Smithsonian Institution Press, 1996.

Bricktop, with James Haskins. *Bricktop*. New York: Atheneum, 1983.

Current Biography, June 1986.

Daniel, Sadie Iola. *Women Builders*. Washington, D.C.: The Associated Publishers, Inc., 1931.

Dann, Martin E. *The Black Press, 1827–1890*. New York: Capricorn Books, 1971.

Editors of *Ebony. The Ebony Success Library* (3 vols). Volume I: *One Thousand Successful Blacks;* Volume II: *Famous Blacks Give Secrets of Success*. Nashville: The Southwestern Company, 1973.

Graves, Earl G. *How to Succeed in Business without Being White*. New York: HarperCollins, 1997.

Haber, Louis. *Black Pioneers of Science and Invention*. New York: Harcourt, Brace & World, 1970.

Haskins, Jim. *Get on Board: The Story of the Underground Railroad*. New York: Scholastic, 1993.

———. *Outward Dreams: Black Inventors and Their Inventions*. New York: Walker and Company, 1991.

Ingham, John N. *African-American Business Leaders*. New York: Greenwood Press, 1994.

James, Portia P. *The Real McCoy: African-American Invention and Innovation, 1619–1930*. Washington, D.C.: Smithsonian Institution Press, 1989.

Johnson, John H., with Lerone Bennett Jr. *Succeeding against the Odds*. New York: Warner Books, 1989.

Johnson, Michael P., and James L. Roark. *Black Masters: A Free Family of Color in the Old South.* New York: W. W. Norton, 1984.

Kaplan, Sidney. *The Black Presence in the Era of the American Revolution, 1770–1800.* New York: New York Graphic Society, 1973.

Klein, Aaron E. *The Hidden Contributors: Black Scientists and Inventors in America.* Garden City, N.Y.: Doubleday, 1971.

LaBlanc, Michael L., ed. *Contemporary Black Biography.* Vols. 1 and 9. Detroit: Gale Research, 1992.

Lee, Spike, with Lisa Jones. *Do the Right Thing.* New York: Simon & Schuster, 1989.

Lewis, Reginald F., and Blair S. Walker. *"Why Should White Guys Have All the Fun?": How Reginald Lewis Created a Billion-Dollar Business Empire.* New York: John Wiley & Sons, 1995.

McManus, Edgar J. *A History of Negro Slavery in New York,* Syracuse, N.Y.: Syracuse University Press, 1966.

Ploski, Harry S., and James, Williams, eds. *The Negro Almanac: A Reference Work on the Afro American.* New York: John Wiley & Sons, 1983.

Reid Merritt, Patricia. *Sister Power: How Phenomenal Women Are Rising to the Top.* New York: John Wiley & Sons, 1996.

Salzman, Jack, David Lionel Smith, and Cornel West, eds. *The Encyclopedia of African-American Culture and History.* New York: Simon & Schuster / Macmillan, 1996.

Smythe, Mabel M., ed. *The Black American Reference Book.* Englewood Cliffs, N.J.: Prentice-Hall, 1976.

Sterling, Dorothy, ed. *Speak Out in Thunder Tones: Letters and Other Writing by Black Northerners, 1787–1865.* Garden City, N.Y.: Doubleday, 1973.

———. *We Are Your Sisters: Black Women in the Nineteenth Century.* New York: W. W. Norton, 1984.

Walker, Juliet E. K. *Free Frank: A Black Pioneer on the Antebellum Frontier.* Lexington: The University Press of Kentucky, 1983.

ARTICLES

Brown, Carolyn M. "The Master of Trades," *Black Enterprise,* June 1996, 253.

"The Buddy System." *The New Yorker,* April 29 and May 6, 1996, 32–33.

Green, Noah. "The Sixth Borough: A Bulletin Board Grows in Brooklyn," *The Village Voice*, July 12, 1994, 1.

Hewitt, John H. "The Search for Elizabeth Jennings, Heroine of a Sunday Afternoon in New York City." *New York History*, October 1990, 387–415.

Kaplan, Michael. "On the Record," *American Way*, October 15, 1995, 48–51.

"The Quiet Man." *The Anthonian*, June 27, 1976, 4–31.

Stout, David. "A. G. Gaston, 103, a Champion of Black Economic Advances." *New York Times* obituary, January 20, 1996, 13.

PICTURE CREDITS

Page 8: Kota funerary figure from Gabon, in Geoffrey Williams, *African Designs from Traditional Sources* (New York: Dover, 1971), 113; page 10: African slave market, courtesy of the Library of Congress, Washington, D.C.; page 13: Captain Paul Cuffe, courtesy of Old Dartmouth Historical Society–New Bedford (Mass.) Whaling Museum; page 18: James Forten, courtesy of the Historical Society of Pennsylvania/Leon Gardiner Collection; page 22: Pierre Toussaint, © collection of The New-York Historical Society; page 26: painting *Free Frank McWorter, Early Illinois Settler,* 1963 oil on canvas by Anna McCullough, courtesy of the DuSable Museum of African American History, Chicago; page 29: African American worker, courtesy of the California State Library; page 32: slave advertisement, courtesy of the Library of Congress, Washington, D.C.; page 37: William A. Leidesdorff, courtesy of the California State Library; page 42: nineteeth-century street scene, public domain; page 48: Union recruitment ad, courtesy of the Chicago Historical Society; page 50: photo of Mary Todd Lincoln, courtesy of National Archives, Washington, D.C.; page 53: Emancipation Proclamation, courtesy of National Archives, Washington, D.C.; page 55: freed slaves, courtesy of the Library of Congress, Washington, D.C.; page 58: Granville T. Woods, courtesy of AP/Wide World Photos; page 64: Madame C. J. Walker, courtesy of Photographs and Prints Div., Schomburg Center for Research in Black Culture, The New York Public Library/Astor, Lenox and Tilden Foundations; page 66: Lelia McWilliams, courtesy of the Library of Congress, Washington, D.C.; page 68: Madame C. J. Walker leaving her home, courtesy of the Library of Congress, Washington, D.C.; page 70: Maggie Lena Walker, courtesy of National Park Service/Maggie L. Walker National Historic Site; page 75: Charles Clinton Spaulding, courtesy of North Carolina Mutual Life; page 80: real estate ad, courtesy of Moorland-Spingarn Research Center, Howard University, Washington, D.C.; page 84: *Underworld* ad, courtesy of Donald Bogle collection; page 87: segregated movie theater, courtesy of Photographs and Prints Div., Schomburg Center for Research in Black Culture, The New York Public Library/Astor, Lenox and Tilden Foundations; page 89: A. G. Gaston, courtesy of the Birmingham (Ala.) Civil Rights Institute; page 94: Ada "Bricktop" Smith, from Jim Haskins's collection; page 98: Native and African Americans, courtesy of the Western History Collections/University of Oklahoma Library, Norman; page 102: Janet Harmon Bragg, courtesy of National Air and Space Museum/ Smithsonian Institution, Washington, D.C.; page 110: Henry G. Parks, courtesy of Archive Photos; page 115: John H. Johnson, courtesy of AP/Wide World Photos; page 118: photo of Johnson with daughter, Linda Johnson Rice, courtesy of AP/Wide World Photos; page 121: 1930s Chicago street scene, courtesy of the Library of Congress, Washington, D.C.; page 125: Berry Gordy Jr., courtesy of AP/Wide World Photos; page 128: the Supremes, courtesy of National Archives; page 131: Quincy Jones, © Jim McCrary; page 136: Earl G. Graves, reprinted with permission of *Black Enterprise* magazine, Earl G. Graves Publishing Co., New York, all rights reserved; page 138: magazine cover, reprinted with permission of *Black Enterprise* magazine, Earl G. Graves Publishing Co., New York, all rights reserved; page 142: Reginald F. Lewis, courtesy of TLC Beatrice International Food, New York; page 148: Oprah Winfrey, courtesy of AP/Wide World Photos; page 152: Spike Lee, courtesy of AP/Wide World Photos; page 157: Alphonse "Buddy" Fletcher Jr., courtesy of Jules Allen; page 161: Omar Wasow, courtesy of Omar Wasow.

INDEX